JOURNAL OF THE
AUSTRALIAN CATHOLIC HISTORICAL SOCIETY
VOLUME 31/32 2010/11

5. Cardinal Moran's arms by Ashwin & Falconer, Cardinal's Palace.

Stained glass by the sea: Cover image 1. Detail of St Bartholomew by John Hardman & Co., Cerretti Chapel.

2. Tower and colonnades of Moran House.

3. St Patrick and St Francis, and right: 4. Our Lady and St Joseph, both windows by Ashwin & Falconer, Moran House.

Stained glass by the sea
Photograph credits: 1, 8: S. Murray; 2, 3, 4, 5, 6, 7, 9, 10, 11: K. Whitmore

Journal of the Australian Catholic Historical Society

Volume 31/32 2010/11

Contents

Journal Editor: James Franklin

Contact

General Correspondence, including
membership applications and renewals,
should be addressed to

The Secretary
ACHS
PO Box A621
Sydney South, NSW, 1235

Enquiries may also be directed to:
secretaryachs@gmail.com

Executive members of the Society

President:
Dr John Carmody

Vice Presidents:
Prof James Franklin
Mr Geoffrey Hogan

Treasurer:
Ms Helen Scanlon

ACHS Chaplain:
Fr George Connolly

Stained Glass by the Sea: St Patrick's Estate, Manly

by Karla Whitmore*

Abstract:

The article provides an overview of the architectural heritage and interiors of the St Patrick's Estate complex, Manly, the Church of Mary Immaculate and St Athanasius, Manly and St Columba's, Springwood. Its particular focus is the identification and description of the overseas and local stained glass windows and the studios that made them. (The images for this article are on the front and back covers.)

St Patrick's College Estate adjoins Sydney Harbour National Park and the North Head quarantine station at Manly on 24 hectares of land granted by the government to the Catholic Church in 1859. The vision of Cardinal Moran, the seminary was intended to become a centre of philosophical and theological studies for all of the dioceses of Australia and worthy of being the Maynooth of the south. Commencing with St Patrick's College (Moran House) and the Cardinal's Palace, both commenced in 1885, the complex was extended in the 1930s with St Therese's Convent and the Cerretti Chapel.

Michael Kelly succeeded Moran in 1911 still favouring the idea of a College as a national seminary but for various reasons, including resource allocation and war, the idea came to an end. In the preceding year the recreation centre (later to become the Cardinal Freeman Pastoral Care Centre) was added at Manly and St Columba's was established in 1909 at Springwood to train missionaries. The parish of St Mary Immaculate and St Athanasius, which was originally included with the seminary, was made independent in 1918 and the present church was established in Whistler Street, Manly, on the site where a church was first built fifty years before. To mark the Eucharistic Congress in 1928 the Blessed Sacrament was taken in procession from Manly to the city on board a ferry, the procession attracting visitors from overseas as well as locals.

Student numbers outstripped accommodation but by the 1960s considerations including decreasing student numbers and increased

* Karla Whitmore is semi-retired after working in administration for a university and associations of firms in the building design professions and as a book editor. She became interested in stained glass windows and their architectural setting several years ago and had an article published in *The Journal of Stained Glass* in London in 2009. This article is refereed.

Journal of the Australian Catholic Historical Society 31/2 (2010/11), 2-14.

maintenance costs eventually led to relocation of the seminary in 1995 to inner suburban Homebush as the Seminary of the Good Shepherd. The former seminary is now the International College of Tourism and Hotel Management. The former Cardinal's Palace adjoins St Paul's School and recent residential development, the pastoral care centre is a café and the convent part of the tourism college. As the land was granted to the church to be held in trust this reuse required the church and participating authorities to consider and resolve rezoning, land management, environmental investigation, any possible archaeological significance and community concerns. Conservation planning for the estate and restoration of the seminary and Cardinal's Palace reflect the heritage value of these sites which are listed on the Register of the National Estate, the State Heritage Register and classified by the National Trust.

Across its buildings St Patrick's has a variety of stained glass by significant firms: John Hardman & Co. of Birmingham in the Cerretti Chapel, St Mary Immaculate Church and St Columba's school, Harry Clarke studios of Dublin in St Mary Immaculate church, Australian studio Ashwin and Falconer in Moran House and the Cardinal's Palace. Other windows indicate the work of two local artist designers.

St Patrick's Seminary
Although considered overly large-scale for the church's needs at the time by Cardinal Moran's supporters, plans were drawn up for an imposing 4-storey building under his personal supervision by the Sydney architects Sheerin and Hennessy whose names are inscribed on the windows on either side of the front entrance. The contractor W.H. Jennings won the tender with a price of £60,000 and commenced work in 1885. John Hennessy (1853-1924) was a noted architect and committed Catholic who trained in England and formed a partnership with Sydney born architect Joseph Sheerin, also a devout Catholic, in 1884. The partnership of Sheerin and Hennessy lasted until 1912 after which Hennessy continued working with his son Jack as Hennessy, Hennessy & Co. and completed Wardell's design for St Mary's Cathedral.

Australian Gothic Revival characteristically adhered to English models and to a less extent European and European influenced English designs. Sheerin and Hennessy's design for St Joseph's College, Hunters Hill, done concurrently with St Patrick's, is closely based on a French Marist

Brothers school and is a 'curious hybrid design, neither Gothic nor Classic'.[1] Hennessy has been noted for a degree of bold experimentation in design, set against an essentially conservative attachment to the mother country, which has produced differing interpretations. The seminary was described at the time as Gothic, of the early French domestic school and according to one report, the Gothic Perpendicular architecture was given 'a slightly Spanish look ... by Hennessy who had practised in Spain and the US'.[2] According to his obituary Hennessy practised for two years in Los Angeles and studied for six months in Spain. The NSW State Heritage Register describes the style as Perpendicular Gothic.

The main feature of the seminary building (Moran House) is its severe dignity with restrained use of decoration which leaves the overall effect to the building's dimensions and proportions. Two tiers of colonnades, (IMAGE 2) a central tower and generous windows are the main features of the front north east aspect. Sheerin and Hennessy were awarded a medal for their designs for the seminary and Cardinal's Palace at the 1886 Colonial and Indian Exhibition in London.

The seminary is built of Pyrmont sandstone and white stone quarried on the adjacent quarantine site. Three steam cranes were used on the seminary building, the tower of which was almost 50 m high. Construction was not without drama; a fatality and a stonemason's strike the progress of which was reported in the *Freeman's Journal* in February-March 1886. Work continued in spite of the dispute with eighty stonemasons employed including non-members of the Co-operative Stonemason's Society. A press report at the time suggesting Shelly Beach should be resumed by the government for public use was vigorously rebutted as an attempt to spoil the church's vision for the site. The foundation stone contained a bottle with several newspapers, coins and a document dedicating the seminary to the glory of God, Virgin Mary, Saints Peter and Paul, St Patrick and St Francis Xavier.

The distinctive features of the front aspect are the Gothic two tiered colonnade and central bell tower above the main entrance above which are carvings commemorating Cardinal Moran, St Patrick and other saints in niches. The interior was intended to be monastic in flavour with black and white tiled ground floor from which a stone staircase supported by columns and arches reaches to the top level. Corridors with Gothic archways and cedar ceilings and rooms with beamed ceilings added to the monastic look. As outlined in detail in contemporary newspaper reports it had 4 classrooms,

rooms and facilities for the rector, 2 reception rooms, refectory and kitchen on the ground floor; cloisters, vice-rector's room, 7 professors' rooms and facilities, chapel and library[3] on the first floor; 47 students' rooms, 2 study halls and oratory in the central tower on the second floor; dormitories, students' rooms and studies on the third floor; and an observation walk behind parapets on the top floor. The servants' quarters had their own staircase and the building was serviced by water tanks on the top level and gas lighting. The belfry was used as an army observation post during World War I.

The light filled interior makes extensive use of kauri and cedar panelling: a large cedar sliding door separates the ceremonial hall, known by the seminarians as the aula maximus, from adjoining lecture rooms. Lifesize portraits of Father Therry and archbishops Polding, Vaughan, Moran, Kelly, Gilroy and Freeman were in the aula maximus. Early paintings, tapestry, sculpture and furniture were set against walls with Victorian stencilled dado, a fragment of which remains on the ground floor, and glass cases on the first floor held historical items. In one corner of the hallway are plaster plaques with Latin inscriptions and Christian symbols reproduced from Roman catacombs. The building has a number of patterned windows with geometric and floral patterns in yellows, greens, blues and clear glass, and extensive use of cathedral glass. Above the main entrance is a small window with Moran's arms and a bullseye pattern cross is above the door opposite the Cerretti Chapel. Two brass plaques listing benefactors of St Patrick's on the first floor are signed 'John Hardman & Co. Birmingham England', the makers of the chapel's windows.

On the first floor above the front entrance the former sacred heart chapel has two 2-light windows which are companion windows to those in the Cardinal's Palace, St Patrick being shown subduing a serpent with his staff. The windows depict Saints Patrick, Francis, Joseph and Our Lady (IMAGES 3 and 4) with more elaborate tracery and cinquefoil windows above. Figures are depicted in clear reds, blues, gold and white against geometric and floral backgrounds and angels in the cinquefoil windows hold banners proclaiming 'Holy, holy, holy'. Inset into doors on either side are more richly coloured patterned windows than the building's predominantly pastel ones. The seminary's windows are by the same studio as those in the Cardinal's Palace which are discussed in detail below. According to an inspection report some of the seminary's windows at one time suffered damage from gale force winds.[4]

St Therese's Convent, on the hill behind Moran House, housed the Sisters of Our Lady Help of Christians who undertook housekeeping for the seminary until 2002 when the order moved to Balgowlah, then closed and the Sisters moved to a retirement village. It was built in 1934 in domestic Edwardian style to a design by Ernest A. Scott of Green & Scott and has brick additions from the 1960s. It is now the offices of the Constellation Hotels group. The original building has a slate roof and copper turret over the former chapel which originally extended to the first floor, later becoming a common room on the ground floor and sewing room and library on the floor above. Early photos show two lancet windows and two smaller hopper ones in place of the current rectangular clear glass windows. Above these a small round window with an angel's head remains in place, also a geometric lancet window on the adjacent west wall. The chapel doorway has an inset glass panel with a red cross on a gold and blue background. The original lancet windows were stained glass[5] and, judging by the angel's head, were possibly by Norman Carter.[6]

The Cardinal Freeman Pastoral Care Centre, now a café, is a single storey building directly behind the tourism college with slate roof and timber columned walkway on three sides and attractive indoor and outdoor courtyards for diners. Kelly House, a brick building linked to Moran House by a walkway, and Gilroy House, beyond the Cardinal's Palace, provided additional accommodation for seminarians in 1954 and 1961 respectively.

Cardinal's Palace

The Cardinal's Palace, later called the Archbishop's House, was designed by Sheerin & Hennessy in domestic Gothic Revival style and built in 1885 by William Farley at a cost of £10,000. According to the conservation management report some aspects foreshadow later nineteenth century architectural elements. White stone quarried on site was used for construction of the two-storey building which has a slate roof with a central turret and gables at either end topped by a Celtic cross. Attractive balconies with cast iron railings featuring Moran's initials and statues of saints adorn the front southern aspect. The stone used was of lesser quality than the seminary to which the building was formerly linked by a carriageway. The ground floor had a large audience chamber cum dining room with black marble fireplace, sitting rooms, large library and private secretary's room. The first floor, accessed by a cedar staircase, had a large council room with red marble fireplace for meetings, oratory (chapel) and bedrooms. Landscape paintings originally adorned the walls. The oratory has a marble alter with four bronze candlesticks and the parquetry floor features the design of the cross. The entrance hall and large rooms have parquetry floors and doors of oak, maple and walnut and cedar joinery is used throughout.

The *Sydney Morning Herald* reported in 1886 that 'there are some very fine stained glass windows in the palace, made by Ash, Wynn and Falconer'[7] which refers to the firm of Ashwin and Falconer. John Falconer came to Australia from Scotland in 1856 after training in London with Alexander Gibbs and William Warrington. Frederick Ashwin came from Birmingham around 1871. The first local professional stained glass designer, Falconer established a studio before forming a successful partnership with Ashwin in the mid 1870s with premises in Pitt Street. Other designers were employed as the firm expanded, notably the first locally trained designer John Radecki who worked with John Ashwin after Frederick's death at J. Ashwin & Co. Ashwin and Falconer was a well-known and prolific manufacturer of windows for churches as well as public and commercial buildings and also installed imported windows.[8]

Contemporary overseas design was emulated at this time in a colony with growing commercial and cultural aspirations and the Gothic Revival style was widely embraced. Designers with training and experience in the United Kingdom contributed to the demand for windows in churches and other buildings. Among their many commissions Ashwin and Falconer designed five windows at St Patrick's Church Hill, three clerestory windows in St Andrew's Cathedral, Sydney, and twelve windows for the dome of Sydney Town Hall. In the 1870s and 80s Ashwin and Falconer provided patterned windows, both vibrant and colourful then more muted and pastel, and figurative windows, mostly small to medium in scale. The repetition of a figure, including variations, in other locations and the heads of saints set in patterned backgrounds are characteristic of this period of the firm's work.

The Cardinal's Palace has patterned windows in the entrance hall and stairwell and first floor hall, a rose window with the Cardinal's coat-of-arms at the top of the stairwell (IMAGE 5), figurative single-light windows with tracery and a tall patterned window with quatrefoils containing portrait heads in the oratory, six rectangular patterned windows with small saints' heads and one with the Cardinal's arms in the downstairs common room, and two round windows the dining room. The windows are recessed into white stone. Those in the entrance hall have geometric floral designs in pastel shades of yellow, pink, grey blue, mauve and brown. Small windows set in door panels feature the sunflower motif, the symbol of the Aesthetic Movement which was first used by Falconer at St Mary the Virgin, Waverley. Above the pastel geometric windows in the stairwell, which are bordered by a clover leaf design, is the cardinal's coat-of-arms in brilliant crimson, blue and gold. The doors at either end of the upstairs hallway feature a Celtic cross.

The Herald considered 'the four windows in the oratory are gems in their way, and deserve special mention for the bold and artistic grouping of colours, as well as for the general design'.[9] The figures of St Patrick, Our Lady, St Joseph, St Canice and St Brigid[10] have finely painted facial features in greyish tones and brightly toned garments. They are set in canopywork and exude a modest charm. The tall single-light window to the left of these windows features quatrefoil patterns with two containing the heads of St Kieran and St Canice (IMAGES 6 and 7), the detailing of whose faces is characteristic of Ashwin. The intricacy of the design is characteristic of Ashwin and Falconer's early patterned windows which have been perfectly described as having 'something Celtic about their intertwining abundance and colouring'[11].

Cerretti Chapel

The Cerretti Chapel was built to a design by Hennessy, Hennessy & Co. (Sheerin having left the practice in 1912), who donated their services. John Nevin, who became rector five years before, was instrumental in establishing the chapel. In order to raise the necessary finance an appeal was set up with a substantial donation in Depression times of £10,000 from Countess Eileen Freehill and this was soon widened to a national appeal. The funds raised for Manly were structured so they could be used for St Columba's as well. The Chapel was dedicated to Cardinal Bonaventure Cerretti, the first apostolic delegate to Australia who died two years prior to the Chapel's opening in late 1935.

The entrance to the Cerretti Chapel is adjacent to the College and the chapel is designed to meld with this building rather than detract from it. It is a single storey Gothic Revival building with a column-free vaulted ceiling strengthened lengthways, flying buttresses and a cluster of chapels at the southern end. The floor is jarrah parquetry with terrazzo in the sanctuary. The pillars supporting the upper sections of the ciborium (baldachino) over the marble altar were initially out of alignment and concerns required an engineering solution which was supplied by J.J.C. Bradfield, the designer of the Sydney Harbour Bridge. The pillars were widened and reinforced with steel struts and the canopy and altar were moved forward 1.5m. Below the windows in the nave are plaster relief stations of the cross. As the chapel was designed for seminarians it has an interior with choir stalls and sanctuary, which is lit by hanging metal framed lights, and five small chapels behind the altar of white, green, grey and pink marble from the Pyrenees which was a gift from Pope Leo XIII to Cardinal Moran in 1887[12]. The organ, originally located at the back of the chapel, is at the back of the eastern choir stalls and further along is the nun's chapel and a tapestry in red, gold and blue.

The windows are by the English firm John Hardman & Co. which started designing and manufacturing stained glass in Birmingham in the 1840s and became a large firm with an international clientele and reputation. The firm designed for St Mary's and St Andrew's Cathedrals, Sydney and St Patrick's Cathedral, Melbourne. Donald Taunton, their chief designer from 1935 to 1964, designed these windows in December 1934-January 1935 with his colleague Vincent Durk and a third designer.[13] The entry in the studio's Day Book for March 1935[14] lists the windows including two rectangular ones designed for the laity chapel which have been relocated to the Seminary of the Good Shepherd at Homebush where they adjoin the entrance. They depict receiving the tonsure and the ordination of a deacon.

The three lancet lights above the gallery and front door comprise the Irish Saints Window depicting St Columba, St Patrick and St Brigid. The original watercolour of this design appeared in Manly in 1936 with the notation 'Block by courtesy of Rev. W. Clark'.[15] St Patrick in the central panel is depicted being called to Ireland while above two angels support the harp of Erin. Immediately above the front door two circular windows depicting on the left the arms of Michael Kelly, Archbishop of Sydney, and on the right Patrick Francis Cardinal Moran with their names highlighted in golden yellow. The apostles and their symbols feature in fourteen single lancet windows on the east and west walls of the nave starting from the choir stalls. They depict Our Lady Help of Christians and Saints Peter, James Major, Philip, Matthew, James Minor and Thaddeus, Joseph, Andrew, John, Bartholomew (IMAGES 1 and 8), Thomas, Simon and Matthias. The first and fourth windows on the east wall are inscribed 'Jacobe' and refers to the St James the Great and the Less respectively. The fourth window on the west wall is inscribed 'James'. Brilliant cobalts, ultramarine and crimson predominate in the garments of the apostles, the features of whom are depicted sympathetically and realistically.

In the sanctuary clerestory are nine small windows of two lancet lights depicting the symbols of the passion including the cock that crowed after Peter's denial. This splendid bird has a red crest and crop, green, pink and mauve feathers and yellow feet. The nun's chapel on the east wall has two small rectangular windows of St Theresa, the Little Flower, and St Paul. Ten small lancet lights are in the ambulatory chapels behind the altar. The Day Book notes that arms of Cardinal Moran and the Sydney Eucharistic Badge were to be discreetly incorporated into windows depicting Our Lady and Christ the King respectively. According to a *Sydney Morning Herald* report of November 1935 the latter chapel originally included a large painting by Norman Carter. All the windows except the circular ones were designed with fixed hopper casements or hopper ventilation.

The appearance of the windows is lighter than as originally installed. In 1951 some of the windows were shipped back to the Hardman studio to correct buckling which was attributed to problems with cementing and with shipping. Double glazing had been recommended and undertaken by John Ashwin, who managed the studio after Frederick Ashwin died, and paid for by the Hardman studio but further deterioration occurred. A report by A.G. Benfield of Frank G. O'Brien Pty Ltd in 1950[16] advised that as well as the cementing problem there was a gap in the glazing. The Hardman studio advised 'outer glazing should always be fixed as close as possible to the painted glass itself, and it should form a complete seal, should not be broken in any way'.[17] In the course of re-cementing they responded to John Nevin's concern about the darkness of tone 'and agreed to substitute lighter toned glass in the more sombre and heavily painted backgrounds'.[18] The larger windows, except the Irish Saints Window, appear to be the windows described. This chapel with its imposingly large and clearly delineated figures in richly coloured windows which are set off by cream coloured walls and ceiling, murals intended for which fortuitously perhaps never eventuated.

Church of Mary Immaculate and St Athanasius

This church in Whistler Street has Romanesque, Norman and Gothic elements and there is Celtic influence in exterior motifs. The original rock-faced sandstone church designed by Tappin, Dennehy and Smart which opened in 1892 was extended in 1908-09 with the addition of transepts, sanctuary and sacristy by Nangle and Nurzey[19] who also designed Holy Cross College, Waverley in Federation Romanesque style. The addition in the 1960s of the front porch and two semi-circular rooms designed as baptistery and mortuary provide the prominent architectural feature of the building's front aspect (IMAGE 10). The interior has a solid vaulted timber roof with trusses, rectangular masonry columns which support the flat roof over the naves and a round arch in front of the sacristy. The gabled slate roof has four crosses plus one atop the small tower. Archbishop Gilroy blessed the completed church in January 1963. Alterations to the interior were also carried out in the 1960s including the installation of a marble altar and the organ was built by Knud Smenge of Melbourne in 1986.

The tall 3-light altar window brings a sense of Gothic lightness to the interior. It is by John Hardman & Co.[20] and dates from 1918. The design was among those taken to Rome by managing director John Tarleton Hardman in 1927. The window was donated by the Wharton-Kirk family; a plaque commemorates Captain Errol Wharton-Kirk who was killed in France in 1914. It depicts a golden haired Blessed Virgin, crimson robed Sacred Heart and green robed St Joseph with elaborate canopywork above the figures. Below are smaller figures of St Bridget, St Patrick and St Columba again with canopywork. The Hardman studio was adept at handling large-scale figures and creating rich and intense colouring.The rose window above the original front door is of pink and clear diamond shaped lead lights and gabled stained glass windows in the transepts from the 1940s are a simple heraldic design with fleur-de-lis in the opening hopper sections.

The windows in the central narthex and former baptistery (now bookshop) and mortuary (now vestry) are signed 'Harry Clarke Studio, Dublin 1962'. Harry Clarke trained in stained glass under Alfred Child and at the studio of Christopher Whall who wrote an influential book on the principles of stained glass manufacture. In 1910 he took over running the firm established by his father Joshua who worked in the area of church interiors. A noted book illustrator as well as stained glass designer Clarke's work was influenced by contemporary artists and designers such as Aubrey Beardsley and the medieval stained glass of Chartres Cathedral. His style has elements of 'eclectic and decadent symbolism of medieval richness and Byzantine splendour'.[21] Clarke's strong vibrant colours set within strong lead lines can be seen in the altar window at St Stephen's Cathedral, Brisbane, the only Australian church with his own work.

Clarke set up a studio in London but his never robust health was failing following an accident in 1926 and the firm operated with the involvement of his family and studio managers. After Clarke's death in 1931 the studio continued until it closed in the 1970s. At the time the church's windows were made it was managed by William J. Dowling. The two-light window in the central narthex depicts Mary Immaculate and St Athanasius with below the ark of the covenant and the monogram Chi Rho. The dove is in a round tracery window above. Three lancet windows in the former baptistery to the right depict Mary in the Temple with Joachim and Anne, the Baptism of Christ and the Presentation of infant Jesus at the Temple with Mary and Joseph. Three lancet windows in the former mortuary depict scenes from the Crucifixion: Mary with the body of Jesus, the Resurrection and Jesus carrying the Cross. The 'illustrative' look is evident in the faces of Mary and St Athanasius and the use of brush marks produces a watercolour feel, particularly in the backgrounds, helped by the use of clear blues, greens and yellows.

St Columba's High School

St Columba's High School is situated at Springwood on 1200 hectares of land originally granted to William Lawson and later owned by Sir Henry Parkes. The original homestead, Elmhurst, and sandstone entrance gateposts are part of the heritage listed site. Building of the seminary in the Spanish mission style by Nangle and Nurzey commenced in 1908 from locally quarried white sandstone. It was opened the following year and commenced operation in 1910 when a news report on the building's progress described it as 'Romanesque'. Extensions continued in the 1920s and 1930s and in 1942 St Columba's became a minor seminary providing secondary education and a year's philosophical studies. The two-storey building of rockfaced sandstone has a central, north and south wing, gabled roof and round arched colonnades on two levels (IMAGE 11). Above the south wing is a tower topped by a copper belfry and cross. The ground floor of the central wing contained a reception room and classrooms while there were dormitories and recreation room on the first floor. In 1960 the cloisters on the eastern side were replaced by a more utilitarian brick chapel and cloisters. Since 1979 the site has been a school which includes agriculture as part of the curriculum. Construction and integration of new facilities with existing heritage buildings is due to be completed in 2012. Fortunately, a fire in December 2010 did not affect the heritage section of the school.

The original chapel, on the western side, was built in 1922 and featured timber fretwork and frames around three rectangular windows originally of clear glass and with choir stalls on either side as in the Cerretti Chapel. The stained glass windows were also designs by Taunton in 1930 for John Hardman & Co.; the designs were sent again in 1935[22] and a photo of them appears in the 1939 *Golden Jubilee Number of Manly*. They depict Mary and the Christ Child flanked by St Columba on her left and St Francis Xavier on her right. Mary is enthroned holding the Christ Child and a golden sceptre with fleur-de-lis, an emblem repeated on the border. She wears a gold and jewelled crown and, as 'Patron Princ Australiae', has the Southern Cross shining above her head. Her robe of intense Hardman blue is contrasted with a red jewelled border and she is framed by a colourful archway of red, greens, gold, deep pink and blue. St Columba kneels facing Mary in a mitre and red robe featuring four images of saints and in the pale blue toned background is the Abbey of Iona. St Francis Xavier also kneels facing Mary wearing a red, brown and olive robe. The windows are signed 'Hardman England'. The windows suffered bowing due to the fierce westerly winds and were restored around 1990 with the addition of a protective Perspex window on the outside to prevent further damage. Three non-figurative windows in the chapel have a red cross on a pale yellow background.

The original entrance doorway has semi-circular windows above the door and in narrow side panels. Curvilinear foliage in variegated green and red borders a red cross. At the top of the cedar staircase is a similar design with gold crosses in a sashed window and adjacent door. These leadlight windows are in the art nouveau style fashionable at the turn of the twentieth century.

In the balcony of the former chapel in the newer eastern wing designed in 1960 by Sidney Hirst, who also designed the extensions to St Therese's Convent, is a round topped window with pale yellow toned background glass. A round insert features the seated figure of St Columba with his staff and one foot extended beyond the circle. Colours are predominantly grey, blue and brown and the folds of the drapery are accentuated by heavy lead lines which also accentuate his intent gaze. In the background are symbols including a sailing boat, dove, thistle and clover. This window looks to be the work of Stephen Moor who studied painting and stained glass in Budapest where he taught art and worked as a stained glass artist. He migrated to Australia in 1950 and later established his studio Ars Sacra at Strathfield. His contemporary designs incorporated architectural use of thick glass set in concrete or epoxy aggregates including dalle de verre (slab of glass). St Peter Julian's church, Haymarket, features his figurative stations of the cross and large colourful abstract windows.

While construction was under way at Manly in the 1880s the *Freeman's Journal* noted the buildings 'assuming an appearance in which the elements of the architecturally picturesque and the religiously romantic are very pleasantly blended'[23]. And so it could be said to remain today for the students and bridal couples who use the facilities. The enduring legacy of St Patrick's Estate is that as well as continuing as a centre of learning the buildings do justice to the setting which inspired a seminary by the sea.

NOTES

1 Morton Herman, *The Architecture of Victorian Sydney* (Sydney: Angus & Robertson, 1964), 76. This quote was attributed to the seminary in an article in the *Catholic Weekly*, 31 August 1988, 12.

2 Quote from the same article in *CW.*

3 The library was moved to Strathfield to become the Veech Library.

4 Extract (undated) from National Trust Women's Committee inspection no. 173.

5 Howard Tanner & Associates, *St Patrick's Estate Vol.2 Conservation Plan* (Surry Hills, 2002), 54. The fate of the four original windows is unknown.

6 Norman Carter was a lecturer in art, portrait painter and designer of stained glass windows including eight clerestory windows for St Andrew's Cathedral (1945-1956).

7 *Sydney Morning Herald*, 24 August 1886, 8, National Library of Australia, http://www.trove.nla.gov.au, accessed 27 July 2010.

8 Other work by John Falconer and by Ashwin and Falconer, and John Radecki, is discussed in detail in the thesis by D. Giedraityte (see note 11).

9 *SMH*, 24 August 1886, 8.

10 The inscription on the common room window of this figure is St Bridget.

11 D.I. Giedraityte, *Stained and Painted Glass in the Sydney area c.1830-1920*, MA thesis, Sydney University, 1982, 405. Since mid 2011 on Sydney University Rare Books Library eResources.

12 Chris Geraghty, *The Priest Factory: a Manly Vision of Triumph 1958-1962 and Beyond* (Melbourne: Spectrum Publications, 2003), p. 11. The second volume of this memoir provides a personal account of the seminary environment.

13 *Time-Sketch Book 2*, Acc 95/77, Birmingham Archives and Heritage, Hardman Archive, MS175. The third designer's initials are FH.

14 *Day Book*, vol. 33 1933-1937, 4 March 1935, Birmingham Archives and Heritage, Hardman Archive, MS175.

15 *Manly*, vol.5, no. 2, October 1936, 27.

16 Kevin Walsh, *Yesterday's Seminary: a history of St Patricks Manly*, (Sydney: Allen & Unwin, 1998), p. 199. Architectural and engineering aspects are included in this official history of St Patrick's seminary.

17 John Hardman Studios to Right Rev. J. Nevin, St Patrick's College, Manly, 13 October 1950. Birmingham Archives and Heritage, Hardman Archive, MS175.

18 JH Studios to Nevin.

19 Spellings vary between Nagle and Nagel, Nurzey and Nurzety. References in the *SMH* 1908-1910 are to Nangle and Nurzey, Architects, 84 Elizabeth Street, Sydney.

20 Listed in The Works of Donald Taunton in and around Sydney, John Hardman Studios, Birmingham, England (undated).

21 Nicola G. Bowe, *The Life and Work of Harry Clarke* (Dublin: Irish Academic Press, 1989), 2.

22 *Time-Sketch Book 2*, London House Estimates Letter Books, vol. 8.

23 *Freeman's Journal*, March 13, 1886, 14.

MARONITE INSTITUTIONAL DEVELOPMENT ACROSS AUSTRALIA

by Margaret Ghosn*

Abstract
Maronites first arrived in Australia in the 1800s and since then have consolidated their presence through institutional structures including churches, schools, childcares and aged care facilities. These developments contributed to the cultural, social and spiritual life of the Maronite community, particularly in Sydney. Although established to cater for Lebanese migrants and their children, today the demands of second and third generations of Maronites have seen the reassessing of these ministerial institutions.

Introduction

The Maronites trace their beginnings to Saint Maroun who led a monastic life in the fourth century in Syria. His way of living attracted disciples. In the fifth century the followers had left Syria to seek refuge in the mountains of North Lebanon where the community grew. However the ecclesiastical organization did not occur until the eighth century when the Maronites became a self-governing (sui iuris) Church with the establishment of the Maronite Patriarchate of Antioch. The Maronite Synod (2003-2006) distinguished aspects of the Maronite Catholic Church as:

firstly, an Antiochene Syriac Church, with a special liturgical heritage; secondly, a Chalcedonian Church; thirdly, a Patriarchal Church with an ascetic and a monastic aspect; fourthly, a Church in full union with the Apostolic Roman See; fifthly, a Church incarnated in her Lebanese and Eastern environment, and the Countries of Expansion.[1]

For centuries Maronites resided mainly in Lebanon. However due to internal conflicts, a significant number of Maronites migrated to Australia. Today we witness a strong Maronite presence particularly in Sydney. The practice of Lebanese culture, maintaining tradition, residential cohesiveness, in-marriages and the strong active presence of the Maronite community is in part due to parishes and educational institutions which have integrated and unified the community.

The following will offer a closer look at the institutions that have supported the growth of the Australian Maronite community over the last century and which continue to remain vital to Maronite identity today.

---

* Dr Margaret Ghosn is a member of the Maronite Sisters of the Holy Family and recipient of the 2009 Australian Catholic Historical Society's MacGinley Award. Her talk on a similar theme was given to the ACHS on 19 June 2011. This article is refereed.

Journal of the Australian Catholic Historical Society 31/2 (2010/11), 15-26.

Settlement of Lebanese Maronites in Australia

In the Lebanese migration to Australia, three periods can be discerned. The first wave occurred between 1880-1946 with the first Maronite family, the Fakhry family, settling in Adelaide in 1854. Many early Maronites who arrived could not speak English and possessed few skills. They became shop keepers, hawkers or self employed entrepreneurs.[2] By 1921 the number of Lebanese-born in Australia was 1803. According to Trevor Batrouney, even with the addition of those Australian born, the Lebanese community during the 'first-wave' period would not have exceeded 5000.[3]

The second mass migration took place between 1947-1974 with many settling in the Parramatta area in search of employment. The Parramatta Local Government 1986 census revealed residents of Lebanese background comprised the largest migrant community, accounting for almost 20 per cent of all residents born in non English speaking countries and the unemployment rate for Lebanese adults was around 27 per cent.

From 1975 onwards, there was the influx of more than 20,000 civil war refugees mostly to Sydney and Melbourne, who were largely poor, and over half of whom were Muslim, transforming the Lebanese community character. According to Michael Humphrey, due to the presence of Muslim Lebanese in Australia and the civil war in Lebanon, greater emphasis was placed on Lebanese Maronite identity across generations, along with increased support of communities back home.[4]

The diaspora today is the product of labour migration, trading activities, flight as refugees from war and economic crisis in Lebanon.[5] Settling in Sydney are 75 per cent of all Lebanese in Australia, with 20 per cent in Victoria and smaller numbers in other States. The strong national concentration in inner west Sydney was the result of long-term chain migration and the establishment of Lebanese institutional structures which assisted integration of Maronites into their own community, thereby reinforcing ethnic identity.[6]

Nationality, Religion and Culture

Data on the pattern of living among Lebanese Maronites in Australia suggests maintenance of Lebanese culture and religion is a priority. Linguistically, according to Burnley, over 92 per cent of Lebanese speak Arabic at home.[7] Furthermore 44 per cent of close relatives reside in the same suburb and there is a great number of return visits to family in Lebanon, resulting in a strengthening of ties and retention of Lebanese values.[8] Improved transport and communication have reduced the social and cultural isolation, experienced by first and second-wave settlers.

Though nearly three-quarters of the second generation marry outside their ethnic group, Birrell and Healy noted that in-marriage for second generation Australians increased in the 1990s for people from the Middle East and was indicated at higher than 60 per cent. This may be due to the size of the communities and the range of services and activities which provide opportunities for meeting people of one's ethnicity and religion.[9]

Religion has also contributed to community cohesiveness. Maronite churches were established and became reassuring institutions for migrants. Abe Ata noted that for Lebanese, religion was equivalent to nationality, and churches provided a vital reference point as far as psychological identity was concerned.[10] What is more, these parishes, established to cater for Maronite migrants, have appeal to second and third generations.

The Development of the Maronite Eparchy in Sydney, Australia

In 1889 the number of Maronites in Sydney was deemed sufficient for the establishment of a Maronite mission. Priests were sent from Lebanon, arriving on 8th May 1893. In 1894 a Maronite chapel was set up in a private house in Waterloo and served the community until Saint Maroun's Cathedral in Redfern was opened and blessed on 10th January 1897 by Cardinal Moran.[11]

From 1963 to 1973, under the direction of Fr Peter Ziade (later Monsignor), an institutional framework was put in place. His focus was to construct a new Saint Maroun's Cathedral and he was assisted by Cardinal Gilroy.[12] The Catholic Weekly edition of 6th May 1965 covered the blessing where 1000 Maronites attended. By 1969 Saint Maroun's Cathedral had an additional hall, school and presbytery. In 1997 the Cathedral celebrated its 100 years.

By 1967 Maronites exceeded 20,000 in Australia, but they had only a few priests, limited resources and were becoming Latinized.[13] In October 1973 Abdo Khalife was appointed the first Bishop. On arriving in Sydney he sought to establish a Maronite Eparchy[14] with the intention to encourage the language, symbols, values, history and tradition, which embody Maronite culture.

Bishop Khalife took up residence at Saint Maroun's Cathedral in Redfern. During his term (1973-1991), he opened Our Lady of Lebanon Church at Harris Park, purchased Saint George Church in Thornleigh and Our Lady of Lebanon Church at Wollongong, purchased a residence at Strathfield which would become the location of the Australian Maronite

Eparchy and commenced construction of a hostel at Harris Park.

In 1991 Joseph Hitti was appointed Bishop. During his term (1991-2002) the Congregation of Lebanese Missionaries (Kriem) commenced their mission in Sydney. In 2002 Ad Abikaram became the third Bishop for the Eparchy of Australia and has continued to service the community with the opening of Mass centres. Whether future bishops should be of Australian birth as they are more in touch with the needs of second and third generation Maronites, has been debated.

To affirm the growing presence of Maronites in Australia the Patriarch of Antioch, Leader of the Maronite Church, Mar Nasrallah Boutros Sfeir, visited Maronite parishes in 1993. He returned again for the 'Maronite 08' event and presided over the Mass held at Parramatta stadium on 13th July 2008. Approximately 20,000 Maronites were in attendance.

Our Lady of Lebanon Church in Sydney

The first Maronite Catholic Church built in Australia was Saint Maroun Cathedral in Redfern. However as many Maronites settled in Parramatta and the surrounding regions, it was necessary that a new church be established there.

In July 1967 the Maronite Catholic Community and Monsignor Ziade purchased 2.5 acres in Harris Park. Plans were submitted with a development application in 1967 based on a photograph from a Church in Brazil, and approval received on 2nd September 1968. It was registered as Our Lady of Lebanon War Memorial Church and School.

The construction site involved deep excavations and continuous pouring for eight hours of over 600 cubic yards of concrete. The daily newspaper reported, 'that its pouring of concrete was a record for one day.' The Church was designed with a circular seating capacity for 1500 people. With the construction beginning to take shape, Maronites offered generous donations.

The foundation stone for Our Lady of Lebanon Church was laid on Palm Sunday 22nd March 1970 in the presence of Mgr Ziade and His Eminence Cardinal Gilroy. Over 10,000 Maronites were in attendance. As construction of the Church continued, the hall was used for Mass and the basement was used by the Maronite Sisters of the Holy Family as a primary school.

The original blue and white statue of Our Lady was seven metres high and made of fibreglass by the sculptor Ron Williams. It was erected on 28th April 1976. However due to objections by neighbours and Council about its size and appearance it was replaced with a five metre bronze statue which was imported from Italy in 1979.

The official opening of the Church took place on 6th August 1978 and today Our Lady of Lebanon is the largest Maronite Parish in Australia and possibly in the Southern Hemisphere, servicing an estimated 30,000 parishioners living in the 50 suburbs around Parramatta. The parish celebrates approximately 350 baptisms and 100 marriages annually and coordinates 20 parish groups.

In 2009 construction commenced for a new four level Community, Youth and Pastoral Centre to serve the needs of all age groups and is set for completion in July 2011. The 4000m2 centre includes rooms for children's activities, Arabic classes, Sunday Liturgy classes, after school groups and tutoring, marriage preparation, parenting workshops, support group for mothers, couples and family counselling, grief support, health and well being education, respite and support groups for carers for the elderly and disabled, recreation room (530m2), drop in centre, library, youth workshops, outreach and charity work, youth counselling and the Youth Worker Project. The parish is not just the provider of faith and spirituality but sought for social and cultural meaning as one parishioner said:

> When you make a particular Church your parish, it's a lot different to attending a Church just for the sake of attending Mass. A parish involves something completely different. It takes it to a new level and that's why I think I've got more of a connection, whether it be in our Lady of Lebanon Church particularly or in other Maronite Churches because there seems to be that same focus, that same kind of activities going on.

Findings in a study by Christopher Partridge noted that despite the modern value of individualism, there remains the significance of a person's sense of belonging to a community with shared values and goals, in which their ideas can be taken seriously, beliefs are verified by others and religiously significant experiences are shared.[15] This finding is supported by what is witnessed at Maronite parishes.

There are many positive contributions by Maronite parishes including services offered to the community and wider society through blood donations, fundraisers, nursing home visit, Vinnies van and other initiatives that continue to bond the Maronites. However there are also shortcomings including the need to cater to 25-35 year olds, greater need of counselling services as divorce, violence and drug abuse increases, greater prison chaplaincy, and finding a balance between progressives and conservatives.

Our Lady of Lebanon Church in Melbourne

The first wave of Lebanese migrants arrived in Victoria between the 1880s and 1920s. Most were males who came to seek their fortunes. By 2008 the Maronite community numbered over 10,000.[16]

Fr Paul El-Khoury arrived on 15th November 1955 and Saint Mark's church in Carlton was rented. In 1958 the Maronite community purchased a former Congregational church in Carlton and on 16th August 1959 it was consecrated as the Church of Our Lady of Lebanon. The Maronite Community, rallied to pay off the loan through fundraisers, door to door collections and generous donations.[17]

In 1967 a house was purchased in North Carlton as a presbytery and centre of the community. The Antonine Sisters set up residence there in 1980 until they built their childcare centre and convent in 1986.[18] From 1987 onwards the community used the Sacred Heart Catholic Church in Carlton as attendance numbers had increased and the Maronite Church was too small.

In 1999 a four acre site was purchased by the community for the development of a new church and centre. The Church of Our Lady of Lebanon in Thornbury was officially consecrated in 2008. In 2010 the parish celebrated 51 weddings of which 18 were Lebanese Maronites married to Lebanese, 105 baptisms, 24 funerals, 56 first Holy Communion participants and a total of 1846 families were registered with the parish.[19]

The Antonine Order of monks arrived on 9th February 1998 to serve the Melbourne community. The monks established their own monastery in Coburg in 2002 to provide spiritual, educational and social services to the parishioners. In 2009 a Mass centre commenced in Dandenong to gather and serve the Maronite community in the outer suburbs.

Other Parishes across Australia

The Lebanese Maronite Order of Monks arrived in Australia in 1970. The first Mass was celebrated in 1972 in a house in Punchbowl. Their church, Saint Charbel in Punchbowl, was completed in 1974 followed by the Monastery in 1987. Saint Joseph in Croydon was purchased and officially opened on 19th December 1978. The new St Joseph's Church was officially consecrated on 19th March 1998. The Maronite community purchased a Latin Rite Church in Thornleigh and consecrated it as the Maronite Church of Saint George. A new Church and hall was built on the existing site and consecrated on April 1st 2001. It celebrated its ten years in 2011. Saint John the Beloved in Mount Druitt under the direction of the Lebanese Missionaries, was officially opened in 2004. Our Lady of Lebanon in Wollongong opened in 1982 with a new church opened on 3rd April 2005. In 2008 efforts began to build Saint Rafqa Church in Austral and in June 2011 plate collections across all Maronite parishes were donated towards this effort.

In 1888 Fr Peter Kairouz was the first Maronite priest in South Australia. Mass was celebrated at Saint Patrick's Church in Adelaide. From 1929 onwards the Maronites had no resident parish priest until 1972. In March 1980, Saint Maroun's Church in Adelaide was blessed and consecrated.

Prior to 1930 the Brisbane parish shared a church with the Melkites. In 1980 Saint Maroun's Church in Greenslopes was established. In 2011 Bishop Ad celebrated Mass at the Gold Coast for hundreds of Maronites residing in the area.[20] In 2008 a Mass centre in Perth was set up with the intention of establishing a Maronite Church and parish. There are also a number of Mass centres and the likelihood of establishing other parishes across Australia in the foreseeable future. Yet Adelaide, Brisbane and Perth have a very small Maronite community and there is a struggle to maintain community spirit. However youth from Perth and mining areas of Western Australia have flown long distances to attend Sydney youth parish functions as have Adelaide and Melbourne youth. There are also youth interstate trips and footy matches between Maronites from interstate parishes.

One witnesses a sense of spiritual rootedness as evidenced from the high level of participation at the Maronite Liturgies and parish events, particularly in Sydney. Monsignor Ziade in the 1960s wrote, 'The most impressive thing I ever saw during my priestly life was the enthusiasm of the Maronite voluntary workers who worked for the Church. The same as their fathers and forefathers in Lebanon.'[21]

Numerous committees have been formed in the parishes and in more recent times a Maronite Radio Station was aired on 1701AM Sydney and later in Melbourne and Brisbane. All these efforts have seen the maintaining of tight-knit communities intent on preserving the Maronite faith, Arabic language and Lebanese culture for future generations.

Maronite Religious Orders and Education

For Monsignor Ziade the need to establish schools was crucial to his work in Australia as he writes, 'We were concerned very much with our schools, for their existence was vital to our survival as a community and to the inculcation in the younger generation of a deep attachment to their country of origin and an abiding respect for good morals and a true Christian faith.'[22] Maronite schools were established from 1970 onwards and their existence has been as ethno/religious-specific schools. Today these schools are experiencing enrolments of children of ex-students, who also insist that their children maintain the religious, cultural and linguistic background.

Saint Maroun and Our Lady of Lebanon Colleges

Fr Ziade invited the Maronite Sisters of the Holy Family (MSHF) to come to Australia from Lebanon. They arrived on 8th October 1968 and established the first Maronite school, Saint Maroun in Redfern in 1970. After a few years the school outgrew its site. The sisters purchased the Carmelite Convent at Dulwich Hill in 1988 and in 1989 Saint Maroun Primary School was relocated. Officially dedicated and blessed on the 11th of March 1989, the College had an enrolment of over 400 students of varying ethnic backgrounds and religious beliefs. As the number of students increased, a high school was completed in 1998.

Our Lady of Lebanon College was opened on January 1st 1973 in Harris Park, Parramatta, under the direction of the MSHF. The College began life with an enrolment of 115 pupils and occupied space under Our Lady of Lebanon Church. The opening of the primary occurred in 1982 by Senator Peter Baume, the Minister for Education. The official opening of the secondary department occurred in 1992 by Prime Minister Paul Keating. The College has 1200 students, the majority of Lebanese Maronite background.

Saint Charbel's College

The Saint Charbel primary school foundation was blessed on 2nd of March 1983. The College opened its doors to students on 1st February 1984 with approximately 100 students enrolled in Kindergarten and Year 1. In 1991 high school classes commenced. The College marked its 25th silver jubilee in 2009 with celebrations focusing on the Lebanese culture and Maronite identity of its 1100 students.[23]

Antonine College

Four Sisters of the Antonine Congregation arrived on 7th October 1980. A Saturday Arabic school was established for the children. In November 1997 the Antonine Sisters purchased the Coburg East Primary School which opened its doors in 1998. The Sisters acquired a secondary school in 2002 in Brunswick the Secondary Trinity Campus and commenced with less than 90 students. In 2005 the Antonine College was formed by amalgamating the primary school, which became known as the Cedar campus, with the secondary school, Trinity campus. By 2006 the Antonine College was offering schooling from Preparatory to Year 12. In 2009 they purchased Saint Joseph campus to cater for growth in student numbers. In 2011 enrolments were over 700.[24]

Pre schools and Childcare centres

The MSHF established the Holy Family childcare centre at Belmore in 1976. In 2001 an extension to the site, so as to cater for 1-5 year olds, was officially opened. A preschool has also been in operation since 1989 at Saint Maroun's College. Plans are currently underway for the sisters to administer a preschool at Our Lady of Lebanon parish. The Antonine Sisters opened a child care centre in Melbourne on 6th November 1986 which has enrolments of up to 80 children.

Tertiary Education

The Senate of the University of Sydney established the Australian Lebanese Foundation in November 2002 to support the development of academic collaboration between the faculties of The Lebanese University and The University of Sydney. The Foundation's brief includes supporting academic, cultural and student exchange between the universities, provision of scholarships and other forms of support to Australians of Lebanese heritage, in order to broaden their opportunities through education.

Elderly Care facilities

Our Lady of Lebanon hostel was completed in 1992 and accommodated 30 residents but due to financial constraints it closed its doors in 2003. The Maronite Sisters of the Holy Family built an aged care facility catering for 50 residents which was completed in 1997 at Marrickville and named Maronite Sisters of the Holy Family Village. It was constructed on the same site as Saint Maroun's College.

In order to meet the increase in demand for this service to the community, the Maronite Sisters commenced in 2006 a new development on the previous existing aged care complex which had been purchased in 1991 at Dulwich Hill. The new aged care facility accommodates 30 high care dementia specific beds and 17 low care beds and was completed in August 2007.

In Melbourne a hostel administered by the Antonine Sisters was opened on 17th December 1995 with 30 beds. A new wing was built in 2006-7 enabling the Saint Paul hostel to offer 60 beds in low care, ageing and dementia-specific.

Maronites have welcomed these aged care facilities as they cater to the linguistic, cultural and spiritual needs of their elderly.

Conclusion

The Maronites arrived in Australia from Lebanon in the late 1800s through migration. What followed was the building of churches and schools from 1970 onwards, a result of the need to maintain religion, culture and language. Throughout these decades the Maronite institutions have become a network for guidance, support and identity. Yet what was once built with humble resources and for a specific purpose can, over time, take on a giant status.

Our Lady of Lebanon primary school was deemed a more than sufficient endeavour by the MSHF in their early years of settlement. This was soon challenged by parents and students, who would withdraw their children if a high school was not built. Saint Charbel, the Antonine College and Saint Maroun all had the same experience. The necessity for K-12 Colleges, constant expansion and updating to be on a par with surrounding educational institutions has now become a reality. Furthermore, the request for further Maronite schools is an ongoing need.

Likewise Our Lady of Lebanon Church, which though built on a grand scale with a seating capacity of around 1500, never imagined it would today cater for a population of 30,000. As a result new additions included the construction of the community, youth and pastoral centre to be opened in 2011. Extra priests (currently 9) have been assigned to the parish. Added Sunday Masses have been timetabled in. These Masses cater for both Arabic and English speaking parishioners. There are also daily Masses in Arabic with the call to provide daily English Mass for the younger generations.

Though being welcomed to Australia and socially and economically settling in, a significant number of Maronites still maintain a cohesive community around these institutions which have taken on a social, cultural and spiritual identity. However whether the Maronite Church in Australia truly enriches the lives of its faithful according to place and times, or whether it is moving towards an ethnocentric Church, is a question worthy of response. As *Gaudium et Spes* dictated:

> How is the dynamism and expansion of the new culture to be fostered without forfeiting loyalty to inherited traditions?... human culture must evolve today in such a way that it will develop the whole human person harmoniously and integrally, and will help everyone to fulfil the tasks to which they are called.[25]

There are challenges that come with being a Church in a foreign country, including nationalistic ties to faith, cultural resistance and the challenge of religious diversity. The Maronite Catholic Church has the role of creating communion among its believers while becoming an expression of the Australian experience which offers new vision, understanding and identity. This will play a role in the future of the Maronite Institutions. Furthermore, as the presence of priests, monks and Religious sisters, who paved the way for the establishment of churches, colleges, child and aged care facilities, decrease in number, the Maronite community will have to rely on the laity to become more visible in the process of maintaining the culture, faith and unity of the community here in Australia.

Bibliography

Ata, Abe W. 'Ethnic Arab-Lebanese churches in Australia.' *Religion and ethnic identity: An Australian Study*, ed. Abe (I.) Wade Ata. Melbourne Victoria: Spectrum Publications, 1988.

Batrouney, Trevor. *Living Our Heritage. The Maronite Catholic Church in Victoria*. Victoria: Hot Gold Printing, 2008.

Batrouney, Trevor. 'Lebanese-Australian families.' *Families and Cultural Diversity in Australia*. Edited Robyn Hartley. Sydney: Allen & Unwin, 1995.

Birrell, Bob and Ernest Healy. 'Out-marriage and the survival of ethnic communities in Australia.' *People and Place* 8, no. 3 (2000).

Burnley, I. H. 'Lebanese Migration and settlement in Sydney, Australia,' *International Migration Review* 16, no. 1 (Spring 1982).

Humphrey, Michael. 'Lebanese Identities: between cities, nations and trans-nations.' *Arab Studies Quarterly* 26, no. 1 (Winter 2004): 31-50.

Maronite Patriarchal Synod. Texts and Recommendations. Lebanon: Bkerke, 2008.

Marounia. Magazine of the Maronite Eparchy of Australia, No. 30, May 2011.

Mikhael, Sayed. *Patriarch Sfeir in Australia. A Journey of Salvage*. Sydney: Ralya Press, 1994.

Partridge, Christopher. 'The Disenchantment and Re-enchantment of the West: The Religio-Cultural Context of Contemporary Western Christianity.' *Evangelical Quarterly* 74, no. 3 (2002): 235-256.

St Charbel's College 2009 Magazine. Silver Jubilee Edition.

Vatican Council II. *Gaudium et Spes*. Austin Flannery, O.P. Editor. N.Y: Costello Pub. Co. 1988.

Ziade, Peter Amin. *Memories and documents of a priest*. The Maronite Diocese of Australia, July 14th 1973.

End notes

[1] Maronite Patriarchal Synod, 'Identity, Vocation and Mission of the Maronite Church,' Text 2, 2006: paragraph 5.

[2] George Dan and the Coorey brothers established warehouses and factories in Redfern. In 1906 a publication for the Centenary celebration of the Municipality of Redfern described George Dan's warehouse as, 'one of the

largest in Redfern, in which over 100 hands find daily employment, all of whom speak in the highest terms of his kindness and generous disposition.'

[3] Trevor Batrouney, *Living our heritage. The Maronite Catholic Church in Victoria*, (Victoria: Hot Gold Printing, 2008), 1.

[4] Michael Humphrey, 'Lebanese Identities: between cities, nations and trans-nations,' *Arab Studies Quarterly* 26, no. 1 (Winter 2004), 47.

[5] Humphrey, 'Lebanese Identities: between cities, nations and trans-nations,' 32.

[6] I. H. Burnley, 'Lebanese Migration and settlement in Sydney, Australia,' *International Migration Review* 16, no. 1 (Spring 1982), 102-103, 109-110.

[7] Burnley, 'Lebanese Migration and settlement in Sydney, Australia', 127, 129.

[8] Trevor Batrouney, 'Lebanese-Australian families', in *Families and Cultural Diversity in Australia*, edited Robyn Hartley (Sydney: Allen & Unwin, 1995), 197.

[9] Bob Birrell and Ernest Healy, 'Out-marriage and the survival of ethnic communities in Australia', *People and Place* 8, no. 3 (2000), 37, 43.

[10] Abe W Ata, 'Ethnic Arab-Lebanese churches in Australia,' in *Religion and ethnic identity: An Australian Study*, ed. Abe (I.) Wade Ata (Melbourne Vic: Spectrum Publications, 1988), 284.

[11] Sayed Mikhael, *Patriarch Sfeir in Australia. A Journey of Salvage* (Sydney: Ralya Press, 1994), 42-45.

[12] Peter Amin Ziade, *Memories and documents of a priest*, (The Maronite Diocese of Australia, 1973), 16, 18.

[13] Ziade, *Memories and documents of a priest*, 133.

[14] Eparchies in the Maronite Eastern Rite are Diocese established outside of Lebanon, headed by a Bishop.

[15] Partridge, Christopher. 'The Disenchantment and Re-enchantment of the West: The Religio-Cultural Context of Contemporary Western Christianity.' *Evangelical Quarterly* 74, no. 3 (2002): 235-256.

[16] Batrouney, *Living our heritage. The Maronite Catholic Church in Victoria*, 4.

[17] Batrouney, *Living our heritage. The Maronite Catholic Church in Victoria*, 19.

[18] Batrouney, *Living our heritage. The Maronite Catholic Church in Victoria*, 22.

[19] Batrouney, *Living our heritage. The Maronite Catholic Church in Victoria*, 73.

[20] Marounia. *Magazine of the Maronite Eparchy of Australia*, No. 30, May 2011, p10.

[21] Ziade, *Memories and documents of a priest*, 27.

[22] Ziade, *Memories and documents of a priest*, 144.

[23] *St Charbel's College 2009 Magazine. Silver Jubilee Edition*, 24-25.

[24] Batrouney, *Living our heritage. The Maronite Catholic Church in Victoria*, 67.

[25] Vatican Council II, *Gaudium et Spes*, ed. Austin Flannery, O.P. (N.Y: Costello Pub. Co. 1988), no. 56.

The Grail - 75 years in Australia: an international women's movement and the Australian Church

by Alison Healey*

2011 marks not only the 75th birthday of The Grail in Australia; it is also the 90th anniversary of the beginnings of the Grail in the Netherlands. I'd like to begin there with a cultural sketch of the Dutch Catholic church in the 1920s and 30s, from which five Dutch Grail women ventured to Sydney in September 1936. (When I speak of culture I'm sure you all understand that I am referring to how people see and understand the world around them and respond to it; the values and meanings underlying what they do and how they communicate.)

I'll then outline the main features of the Australian church culture they encountered. What was their response? What kind of reception did their initiatives receive? I'll use a couple of particular experiences in Melbourne and in Sydney (the first in the 40s, the second in the late 50s) to illustrate the inevitability, I believe, of conflict between The Grail and Australian church authorities, given their different world views and understandings of 'church'.

This will bring us up to the decade of the 1960s, made notable by Vatican Council II and widespread cultural change in the church, despite efforts to contain it.

The rest of my presentation will sketch, with the broadest of broad brushes, a few images of The Grail at work from the 1960s till now.

My aim here is simply to offer a few lines of thought about the Grail that you may like to consider and that may prompt some discussion and questions.

I've brought a simple leaflet which summarises the Grail in Australia today. I've also listed some sources I've used: works of history by Marjet Derks in the Netherlands, and Edmund Campion, Sally Kennedy and Patrick O'Farrell in Australia, together with Grail archival material.

Dutch church in the 1920s and 1930s
In 2007, Derks, a woman historian at Nijmegen University, Netherlands, published a book on the Dutch church of the 1920s and 1930s which brought

---

* Alison Healey writes on religious, cultural and historical topics including 'A critical alliance: ABC religious broadcasting and the Christian churches (1932-1977)', *JACHS* 26 (2005), 15-28, and has also held various roles in The Grail. This is the text of a talk to the Australian Catholic Historical Society on 10 Apr 2011.

Journal of the Australian Catholic Historical Society 31/2 (2010/11), 27-38.

27

fresh insights into that period of church history, resulting from her close study of lay women who rose to the challenge of revitalising Catholic life and mission in the world. The accepted view of the Dutch church has been that, between the two World Wars, it was a complacent community, turned in on itself, traditionally conformist, anti-modern; and that the tensions between religion and modernity surfaced abruptly in the Netherlands in the 1960s. Not so, says Marjet Derks, there were critical and radical Catholics challenging and stirring this routine-run church and making their mark with energy and passion decades earlier. Whereas the contribution of men was principally in writing and discourse, the women expressed their criticism in a radical embodied way. Derks focuses particularly on two lay women's groups, both founded by Jacques van Ginneken (1877-1945), a Jesuit scholar at Nijmegen University with an international reputation in linguistics and philology, who was also well read in the related fields of anthropology and sociology. Van Ginneken called these two groups he inspired the Ladies of Bethany (1919) and the Women of Nazareth (1921). The Ladies of Bethany, to his disappointment, became a religious congregation in 1932. The Women of Nazareth succeeded in maintaining and strengthening their lay status and ethos and eventually became known as The Grail, for reasons I'll explain.

Van Ginneken was very critical of Northern European society post-World War 1, with its growing secularism and marked by the moral consequences of war; and he was equally very critical of rigid, lukewarm Catholicism in the face of these realities. Derks connects his radical thinking with that of Leon Bloy and Jacques Maritain in France and with John Henry Newman and GK Chesterton in England. Van Ginneken's alternative vision was of a deep, vigorous, passionate Catholicism drawing inspiration from early Christianity. Unlike most of his contemporaries, he believed that women could best embody this vision. While he was critical of aspects of modernity, he was not anti-modern. On the contrary, he wanted his radical Catholics to embrace all the resources modernity afforded to achieve what Derks calls their 'restorative religious' aim. His modernity was evident also in his criticism of power relations.

The first Women of Nazareth formally began their life together on November 1, 1921. The Feast of All Saints seemed then, and still seems, a most appropriate Foundation Day. They entered into a strong program of spiritual formation – theology, scripture, liturgy, prayer and contemplation – and discipline; and made a formal dedication of their lives for nothing less than the 'conversion of the world'. Van Ginneken gave them conferences on strong women in the Scriptures and in the history of Christianity: he developed a kind of female genealogy to help them develop an identity and, as it were, legitimate their life orientation. The names, Women of Nazareth, Ladies of Bethany, are signs of this formative process.

In the first years, the group decided on two approaches to their goal: locally they went to work in factories to renew Catholic faith among working girls there; internationally, they sent 3-4 of their people with postgraduate university degrees to Java intending to establish a dynamic Catholicism among university women there that would reach out to other parts of Asia. (This project did not go ahead but The Grail maintained a different kind of presence in Java through to the 1970s with later personnel drawn not only from the Netherlands but also USA, Australia, Philippines and Portugal.) However, in 1928, the Bishop of Haarlem expressed his wish that the Women of Nazareth take responsibility for recruiting, leading and forming a nation-wide movement of Catholic girls. This was a huge change of direction, but van Ginneken urged them to accept it. He gave the name 'Grail' to this girls' youth movement and over time, the title 'Women of Nazareth' dropped away. All involved came to be known as Grail members, and the Women of Nazareth among them were identified, when necessary, as Grail Nucleus members. The Grail movement in the Netherlands became an outstanding and expressive mass movement of girls. By 1932, after three years, there were 23 Grail Centres in the cities, 700 branches in villages and towns and 8000 members. By 1941 before the German occupation, when The Grail was proscribed by the Nazis, 21000 girls had joined.

I want to return to the fact that van Ginneken urged the group to take its direction from the Bishop. Independence of decision-making has always been cherished in The Grail. Van Ginneken insisted on the necessity of remaining a movement of lay women, as free as possible from controlling power structures in the church that inhibited their flexibility to move and act and change according to needs and circumstances as they saw them. However, he didn't underestimate the power of masculine authoritarianism and he constantly advised the Grail Nucleus to avoid frontal confrontation with bishops as much as they could and try to find more subtle ways of maintaining the integrity of their lives and purpose.

So, all that I have said of the church in the Netherlands, about J. van Ginneken's critique of, and vision for, society and the church and the first 15 years of activity of the Dutch Grail was the formative context out of which the 'first five' Dutch women arrived in Sydney in 1936. They were confident in their identity, their spirituality, their vision of the church in the modern world. With a background of creative initiative and effective organisation, they were mission-oriented, and ready for action. They were welcomed by bishops, priests and laity in large numbers with great enthusiasm and, on the whole, very little understanding.

Meeting the Australian church

The Australian church culture they encountered in Sydney was strongly influenced from Ireland, even though the Manly Union of priests had been promoting native clergy and leadership since the 1920s, with Rome supporting this policy. Not that Australian leadership, when it happened, changed the culture much. It was a church that was masculine and generally non-intellectual, that emphasised individual and family piety and devotion with occasional public devotional processions, Catholic community cohesion under the authoritarian rule of bishops and priests, an unremitting expectation of lay obedience to clerical instructions. However, a significant number of Australian Catholic women within this dominant church culture obviously had other aspirations, because the Grail group had speedy success attracting women to their vision for women's involvement in a dynamic church. In 3 years there were 1000 young active Grail members in Sydney alone, and the Grail movement had stimulated a lively and remarkably enduring response among women and girls in Melbourne, Brisbane, Adelaide, New Zealand, and regional centres in NSW, Victoria and Queensland. Clearly, the Grail's arrival here was timely. Sally Kennedy and Ed Campion have both written about the lay women's organisations that preceded The Grail in Australia and, sharing similar ideals for women, gave The Grail their friendship and support. There were also religious women in a number of congregations that warmly did the same.

This brings us to the end of 1939, three years of immensely hard but flourishing work in Sydney. There had been times when the Grail leaders had had to assert themselves in the face of misguided expectations, but they were able to do this without serious ill effects. On the other hand, they remained a dubious proposition for many clergy, because of their evident desire to be free of clerical interference in their lives, eg, resisting any moves by the bishop to impose a priest chaplain or spiritual director. Let me be clear: Grail women have always sought knowledge and guidance and inspiration from beyond The Grail but have always wanted to be able to choose those sources themselves.

Changing the tone now, I want to give a short account of two crises The

Grail faced – in Melbourne in the 1940s and in Sydney in the 1950s, both of which threatened the continuation of Grail work in these two cities. In the event, the Grail emerged, certainly not unscathed, but intact – for different reasons. Of course, there were personality factors on both sides involved in the conflicts, but most basically they resulted from a clash of cultures.

Melbourne crisis
The Melbourne church under Archbishop Daniel Mannix was a little different from Sydney: more liberal, more hospitable to intellectual thought. Mannix's authoritarian leadership was not as narrow as that of Archbishop Kelly, or his successor Norman Gilroy. In 1940, The Grail accepted his invitation to live and work in 'Tay Creggan', a Tudor-replica house set in a large garden in Hawthorn, owned by the Archdiocese. This gave the Grail women an opportunity to take another approach. Instead of creating a mass movement of girls resourced through short-term formative programs and activities, as they were doing in Sydney, their hearts were set on a 6-month residential course for young women, in which the religious, cultural and social dimensions of Christian life could be integrated in a way of life in community. With no money, but some persuasive friends, they got a bank loan and built dormitory accommodation for 48 and a large all-purpose hall. They called the course 'The Quest' and young women came not only from Victoria but from interstate and New Zealand, some paid for by their parents, others identified as potential youth leaders funded by dioceses, parishes and other interested groups. Still girls in Melbourne parishes were not neglected. The Grail leaders were asked to undertake the work of stimulating and resourcing some existing girls' groups. The National Secretariat of Catholic Action had been set up in Melbourne in 1937 under the leadership of Frank Maher. Frank was a founding member of the Campion Society of laymen (1931), who, like the Grail, sought a dynamic Catholicism open to the world. In following years, the Secretariate, oversaw the setting up of Catholic Action organisations under the direction of clergy, for young workers, students, girls and rural Catholics. All Catholic girls were urged to join the NCGM and initially The Grail was asked to take responsibility for the training and formation of leaders.

But, as time went by, tensions grew between the priest directors of Catholic Action and The Grail. There were underlying differences of approach: central management and centrally defined goals on the one hand and, on the other, a preference for encouraging individual creativity and providing a more flexible environment for young women to discern their own action as Catholics. Some girls preferred the latter and remained members of the Grail movement, which did not please some of the Catholic Action priests. But more than this, a group of the priests wanted the resources of 'Tay Creggan' to be put fully at their disposal; they objected to The Grail's having 'privileged' use of the property and made strong representations to the Archbishop to place it under diocesan clerical management. The Grail leaders appealed to Archbishop Mannix, who decided in their favour. I do believe that the work done there in the ensuing decades vindicated his judgment and I think he believed so, too. But relations with those priests were never repaired. It was 20 years later when I met one of them and was sad to find that he was still bitterly resentful that that decision went against him. Patrick O'Farrell records something that Vincent Buckley remembers Archbishop Mannix saying to him on one occasion: 'If you are ever attacked, as you think, unfairly, come to me. I will see you are not wronged'. He certainly acted in this way towards The Grail in the 1940s. And he remained a benevolent figure in our lives in the years following.

The Grail owned no property in Melbourne, so the loss of 'Tay Creggan' would have meant having no base there to work in, or from. It was a fearful time. We were better placed, with a house of our own in Sydney, when we incurred the wrath of Cardinal Gilroy in the late 1950s.

Sydney library crisis

It was in 1950 exactly, that The Grail in Sydney accepted the invitation to take responsibility for the Southern Cross Library, an initiative of the Knights, then housed on the first floor of Pellegrini's in George Street. It was a relatively small holding of books, (according to Patrick O'Farrell, ¾ fiction compared with the Melbourne library with ¾ non-fiction). The goal for the Grail team there was to build up the holdings in a range of non-fiction areas, increase the number of borrowers and try to make the library a stimulating place to visit. Catherine Bagley and Philippa Green were the initial staff, supported by volunteer Grail members. They subscribed to the main current Christian journals in English; for two years, Philippa fronted a ½ hour program on books on 2SM; they began inviting attractive speakers to the library, including overseas visitors.

In 1953, the library, now with 15,000 books, was moved to the ground floor of CUSA house in Elizabeth Street – a so much more attractive and larger and readily accessible space. The range of books and journals increased further, the speakers' program continued (James McAuley gave first readings of some of his most famous poems there); in the first six weeks there were 300 new borrowers; another full-time staff member joined the Grail team, the volunteer program increased.

The Grail staff could only ever take a very small stipend from the library and the Grail funded Philippa's postgraduate course in librarianship; it was clear the library needed some other source of subsidy and they came up with the idea of opening a bookshop in conjunction with the library to help finance it. This proposal ran up against a counter-proposal from the Archdiocese that EJ Dwyer take over the whole of the ground floor of CUSA for a bookshop and religious artifacts and that the library move upstairs to a space that could accommodate only 1/3 of the existing library holdings. It was the Cardinal's expressed wish that The Grail continue to take responsibility for the library in these new circumstances. This was to happen in 3 weeks. It is hardly necessary to say that the Grail women who had given their all to the project of the library were crushed.

The National President at the time, Adelaide Crookall, said 'No' to the Cardinal's 'expressed wish', she could not countenance committing Grail personnel to such a desolate future after all the creative, constructive work they had done. This failure in obedience was not an experience Cardinal Gilroy relished at any time, least of all coming from a lay women's movement and some correspondence took place. Throughout the exchange of letters, Adelaide was counselled by the then Apostolic Delegate, Archbishop Carboni, who gave his diplomatic skills to guiding her responses. She set out the vision of the library supported by a bookshop and pleaded for support for the further development of what had become a lively centre of thought and exchange. Catholic writers frequented the library; seminarians keen for contemporary material from overseas devoured the journals; the library had become important to a lot of people, city and country dwellers. But the Archdiocesan mind was made up (don't forget the bishops' financial interests in EJ Dwyer) and Cardinal Gilroy was very angry with The Grail for walking away from the Library. He said he could approve no future role for the Grail in the Archdiocese and would instruct his priests to give The Grail no support. [Only this week I learnt from Philippa one further detail about the last days in the Library, which made us both laugh. After the books were culled to the number that would fit upstairs, Philippa put in a few more months' work there and, on her last day, a priest gave her 'some money to buy a couple of pairs of stockings'.]

Consequences of library decision
Well, the Cardinal had spoken, but we had some friends among the clergy

who remained so and, with a house in North Sydney, thanks to a generous benefactor, Mrs Collins, we had a secure home. It was a blow to lose the library with its possibilities for nourishment of the Christian community, but there were plenty of other things to do. Catherine and Philippa gave much of the rest of their working lives to teaching in Africa and Fiji respectively, and enriching our perspectives here in the process. Margaret McCristal moved back to Melbourne, where she joined the staff of the Catholic Library and Bookshop in another Elizabeth Street, eventually becoming the bookshop manager and developing there what had been the dream for Sydney. Other Grail Nucleus members in Sydney also moved to Melbourne to launch a new Adult Education project there, which at its peak through the 1960s brought close to 1000 women and men to evening courses. One Grail Nucleus member remained in the Sydney Centre to focus on accommodating the needs of young women students, particularly Asians, and continuing to resource the growing Family Apostolate Movement, an initiative of married Grail members in 1952. It was only in 1971, after the installation of Cardinal Freeman, that The Grail took up a more public stance again in Sydney.

It was not long after our conflict with the Cardinal that Adelaide Crookall, on her way by road to Queensland, called in to see Bishop Edward Doody in Armidale who had invited The Grail to work in his Diocese. At a certain point in the conversation, he said bluntly to Adelaide, 'The Grail has been in Australia for over 20 years, what have you achieved in that time?' Adelaide without hesitation replied, 'We have survived, My Lord'. It was not an answer he expected, but it was clear he understood her. There was a wrinkling around his eyes - a hint of a smile - 'So you have', he said, 'so you have'.

Cultural change inthe 1960s
Cultural change swept through the Catholic church from the 1960s as a result of strong cultural movements in modern Western societies and the Second Vatican Council which opened the church to the modern world. In the Australian church, changes were both welcomed and embraced and struggled with. With all the complexities that entered into the life of the church from that time, church authorities have had so much else to absorb their attention and energy that The Grail has been able since to pursue its goals, not entirely smoothly, but without the crises of earlier times. We also seemed more normal after Vatican II. Maria de Lourdes Pintasilgo, founding member of the Grail in Portugal, leading feminist and politician (caretaker Prime Minister for a time), gave a televised interview in the 90s

in which she was asked to reflect on the impact of Vatican II on The Grail. 'Well', she replied with a disarming smile, 'it was affirming. We said, "Look, what we have been doing, now they say it's OK."' There were many others at that time who would have said much the same thing.

Other images of the Grail at work

Mackay

I have spoken so far with a particular emphasis on Sydney and Melbourne, but I must also say something about two other centres of Grail activity in Queensland. Bishop Tynan in Rockhampton, invited The Grail to set up a centre in Mackay and in 1956, two Grail Nucleus members went there to open a residential centre for working girls needing accommodation in the city. From the beginning, 'Ballybrac' was understood by the Catholic community to have a claim on their practical support. In the more than 30 years of its existence, it became a regional centre of Christian life and mission, where the Grail team worked on a number of cooperative projects with the Catholic community, members of other churches and other Mackay citizens: social development projects, actions for social justice, adult education programs, training of catechists, preparation for marriage courses and a family movement.

Townsville

In 1964, The Grail responded to another invitation from Queensland., this time from Bishop Ryan, in Townsville. We accepted responsibility for a Catholic Women's College, affiliated with James Cook University of North Queensland, another welcome project with young women, this time university students, a number of whom were girls from farms and small towns and the first generation of their families to have tertiary education. Committed as we were to women's development of their potential, we did our best to help them achieve their goals and, at the same time, shape with them in St Raphael's College an engaged Christian community. We were well-placed, too, to play our part in ecumenical activities on campus and in town, and collaborate with university staff in various ways. There was one battle we had to fight repeatedly there, however – the independence of the Women's College. It was a condition for our accepting the task in the first place. We wanted women to take all the leadership roles in a College, to be the initiators, the representatives, the organisers, the public speakers - to become confident in themselves and their abilities. Yet, for 35 years we were always only temporarily free of pressure from the men associated with St

Paul's Catholic College next door, to become subject one way or another to their management While there were some priests involved, most of St Paul's College Council were laymen, so this was not a clerical-lay conflict like those I've described earlier in Melbourne and Sydney. This was about male dominance of women, a much more wide-ranging phenomenon.

Private association of Christ's faithful

A friend visited me this last week from Christchurch and told me that she had googled The Grail, in some way I haven't been able to replicate, and got an official Catholic Church website, with the single entry of The Grail, which was briefly described. At the bottom of the page there was a statement to the effect that this organisation 'does not speak for the church'. In that context, it read like a particular cautioning about The Grail and she wondered what we had done to deserve this special mention. I'd like to explain the context for this disclaimer. According to earlier Canon Law, The Grail had the status of a pio unio (a 'pious union'). These days we are one of the Associations of Christ's Faithful, of which there are two categories, 'public' and 'private' - not, I think, well-chosen terms. 'Public associations' are those established by a decision of the Holy See (international), an Episcopal Conference (national) or a Bishop in his own diocese. All other Associations of Christ's Faithful are designated 'private' and have no authority to speak for the Catholic church. I assured my friend that we were not a particular target for this disclaimer; that we never had, were never likely to have and never wanted to have the status of an association mandated by the hierarchy to speak their mind.

Australians overseas

It was only in preparing this talk that I really took stock of the contribution of Australian Grail women in other parts of the world. You will remember that at its beginning, the 'conversion of the world' was the Grail's vision. With the development of the theology of the 'kingdom of God', the 'transformation of the world' is how people speak now. I now realise that, adding together all the years of living and working with people of other cultures in other lands, Australian Grail members have collectively given well over 100 years of their energy and creativity and hope in Asia (Hong Kong, Vietnam, Indonesia, Singapore, India, Thailand and Cambodia), in the Pacific (PNG, Solomons and Fiji), in Africa (South Africa, Uganda, Ghana and Tanzania). In PNG, there is now an indigenous Grail movement of women in 5 provinces, recognised as a national entity in the International

Grail and developed and developing in close association with us in Australia.

Cultural change in the Grail

I spoke earlier of the widespread cultural change that permeated the church from the 1960s. The International Grail, of which we are a part, has changed a lot over the years, too, so a few final words about cultural change in The Grail. This is no thorough analysis, just a few thoughts that come to mind.

- Where the Grail Nucleus once led the movement, progressively leadership at all levels in The Grail was more widely shared. We had always affirmed the equal dignity and worth of all vocations, we needed to embed this in our structures. So, from the 1960s onwards, any Grail member, with the necessary capacities and availability, may be elected to any role.

- Once The Grail had put down roots and had local membership in countries in Africa, South America and Asia, as well as Europe and North America, it needed to hear the voices from those diverse cultures in policy and decision-making. This was guaranteed in new structures in 1967, reducing the dominance of the largest Grail entities in Europe and USA. Australian made a major contribution to this change, which had an immediate and lasting impact.

- In the early 1970s, Grail women in Brazil, Mexico, Costa Rica and Portugal particularly brought into the International Grail liberation theology in practice, with its focus on justice, the conscientisation of the poor and working for change from the base. This was a whole new perspective on the world and on Christian mission in it. Paolo Freire's educational philosophy and methodology was taken up widely in the 70s and continues to be the foundation of many effective Grail programs for cultural and social change.

- The movement for Christian ecumenism began to change The Grail from the 1970s. In various countries, Grail women were active in the ecumenical movement; two, one from Belgium and the other an Italian from Switzerland, worked for many years in the Secretariat for Christian Unity in Rome. In the USA, close relations developed with women from Christian churches other than Catholic to a point where some of these wanted to become part of The Grail. And this has been gradually occurring elsewhere also. In the 90s a group of young Swedish women who had participated in European Grail programs, mentored particularly by the Portuguese, asked for recognition as a Grail group. This was different from individual women here and there joining existing Grail groups. After prayer and discernment in all the Grail groups, the decision was made to welcome them. My judgment is that our faith has been strengthened by the presence of these women from other churches in our midst and we are surely being challenged to go more deeply into what Christian unity demands of us. While Catholics still predominate, in the late 90s we took the decision internationally to describe The Grail as a Christian movement.

There other influences that have changed, and are changing, The Grail's view of the world and the church and its own identity, eg:

- Reading the Scriptures through women's eyes, feminist theology and the movements in society and church advocating for women;

- Other theologies exploring the meaning of the 'kingdom of God', God's presence in the whole of creation; the relationship of other world religions to Christianity.

These changes have all come from the founding imperative of The Grail to 'embody the vision' of a vigorous Catholicism engaging with the world. The vision may be advanced through study and writing, but van Ginneken's desire was that, most of all, The Grail would live it. It's a challenge that we've at times risen to and at times failed to meet. I decided, since it's our 75th anniversary, not to dwell on our failures this afternoon. And ask your indulgence of this. Mind you, Jacques v Ginneken once said that The Grail could accomplish its purpose in 75 years, providing that Grail women were full of the love of God and were wholly committed to the task. Judged by that standard, the very fact that I'm standing here at all this afternoon is evidence of failure in a big way. This is the time to stop talking and sit down.

References
Edmund Campion: *Australian Catholics: the contribution of Catholics to the development of Australian Society*, Viking 1987.
Marjet Derks: *Heilig Moeten: Redicaal-katholiek en retro-modern in de jaren twintig en dertig.*, Hilversum 2007. (tr. *Holy should*, or *Be holy* - the imperative to be holy').

Grail Archives
Sally Kennedy: Faith and Feminism: Catholic women's struggles for self-expression', *Studies in the Christian Movement* 1985.
Patrick O'Farrell: *The Catholic Church and Community: An Australian history*, NSW University Press, Revised Edition, 1985
(*Note* error p.386, corrected in S Kennedy's research and in the following publication.)
Patrick O'Farrell: *The Irish in Australia*, NSW University Press, Revised Edition 1993.

A History of the Catholic Bushwalking Club

Peter Blayney*

Introduction

I wish to acknowledge the written works of long serving Catholic Bushwalking Club member, Jim Barrett. He has written eleven short works on the CBC and its connections to the Blue Mountains. For this talk I have relied heavily on his latest book, *Through the Years with the Catholic Bushwalking Club.*[1] However, my interpretations of people and events in this talk are my own.

The Sydney priest whose name was and still is associated with the Catholic Bushwalking Club (hereafter CBC) is that of Father Richard Bede Coughlan. His obituary in The Catholic Weekly of July 1979 had this to say:

> His ability to lend a sensitive and attentive ear to people's troubles came partly from the sense of calm he gained as a bush lover with the Catholic Bushwalking Club he co-founded in 1943 and was chaplain of until 1963.[2]

There are several points to make here. It is generally agreed amongst former and current members of the CBC who knew him that he did listen well to people, that he gave them much time to speak of their problems or concerns, material, spiritual or otherwise. It is said by some that, as a man of firm beliefs and principles, he was rarely swayed from his own point of view. He had less of the collaborative style of leadership and far more of the clearly directional.

He was definitely a bush lover for he had found solace and peace in the natural environment all his life. He was an early example of what has become known as the "bushwalker". Believe it or not, there is a history in this country on this topic too. A recent work is one example: *The Ways of the Bushwalker On Foot in Australia.*[3]

The obituary said he was co-founder of the CBC in 1943. He was its first official chaplain from 1944 to 1963. If he were the co-founder, who was his partner or partners in this venture? This leads me onto the first major point, to examine how the CBC was formed.

---

* Fr Peter Blayney was ordained in 1979. He holds an MA (hons) from Macquarie University. He is the Judicial Vicar of the diocese of Parramatta, Parish Priest of Guildford, and Chaplain to the Catholic Bushwalking Club. This is the edited text of a talk given to the Australian Catholic Historical Society on 12 Sept 2010.

Journal of the Australian Catholic Historical Society 31/2 (2010/11), 39-52.

39

The Early Days of the CBC

It is now recognised within the CBC that it was Miss Dorothy Clayton who, with a few friends, was the key person in the establishment of the Club. In fact, Dot Clayton comes before Fr Coughlan. She sent out a circular dated 31st July 1943 inviting people to a meeting on Wednesday 11th August, 1943, at 8pm, at the 'Cooperative Service Rooms' in George Street, Sydney. It was addressed to 'all who are interested in the formation of a Catholic Bush Walking Club'.[4]

Dorothy Clayton was born in Sydney in 1913. She was ten years younger than Fr Coughlan. In 1929 she found herself in England where her father was sent to work in his company's London base. After leaving school she worked in an office where she met a girl who was a member of the St Francis of Assisi Catholic Ramblers. Dot joined the Ramblers in 1938. The club combined walking and devotional activities such as visits to Marian shrines. She returned to Australia in 1939. Dot wrote an article in the November 1942 edition of *The Fireside*, the magazine of the Legion of Catholic Women,[5] where she hoped something similar to the Ramblers could be established in Sydney. One reader of the article was Catholic layman Paul Barnes who was a member of the Sydney Bush Walkers, a club formed in 1927.

In February 1953, *The Catholic Weekly* reported that the CBC commemorated its tenth anniversary of the first walk on 14th February 1943. A formal dinner and dance was held at the Coronet Ballroom with 120 people present. The report says,

> The president, Mr Lew Garrett, and secretary, Miss Marie de Mol, received the official guests, who included the chaplain, the Rev. Father R. B. Coughlan, and Miss Dorothy Clayton, whose article in *The Fireside* of November 1942, inspired the formation of the Club.[6]

On the occasion of the CBC's 40th anniversary in 1983, Dot Clayton summarised the beginnings of the Club. She, Paul Barnes and another foundation member, Joe Lyons, met with Father Albert Thomas (later Bishop of Bathurst) in 1943 as he was in charge of the emerging and very new adventure within the Church, the Lay Apostolate. The trio said they were forming a club but wanted a 'Spiritual Director'.[7] Club minutes show that the word 'chaplain' was used[8] for the first two years. In amendments to the Constitution in 1948, the term 'Spiritual Director' was used a title by which the club chaplain was known until very recent times.[9]

Dot's recollection is that at that very meeting, Fr Thomas telephoned

Fr Richard Coughlan, then Bursar of St Patrick's College, Manly. He was well-known as a "bush lover" and very interested in walking. According to Dot, Fr Coughlan had been thinking of forming such a club but did not want people to be involved in an activity which might make them miss Sunday mass.[10] The Minutes of the Committee meeting for 9th May 1944 contain a one line note saying, 'Announced that Fr Thomas had indicated he has a chaplain in mind'.[11] In fact, even before Fr Thomas was involved, Father (later Cardinal) James Freeman (then Archbishop Gilroy's Private Secretary) was approached to have the fledging club recognised as a Catholic organisation. Father Freeman referred the matter to Father Thomas as he was the Director of the Lay Apostolate. At the Club's second general meeting on 8th September 1943 Father Coughlan was present at the invitation of Father Thomas. At this meeting a draft Constitution was agreed upon for submission to Archbishop Gilroy.

At the meeting of 10th November 1943, it was announced that the Archbishop had provisionally accepted the Constitution. Full approval was not given for a further twelve months. Approval was finally granted which coincided with the appointment of Father Richard Coughlan as official chaplain on 6th December 1944.[12] He is first mentioned as such in the Committee Minutes of 3rd January 1945. With his appointment, the Catholic Bushwalking Club became an officially recognised Catholic body. The minutes contain no explanation or comment on the new official member of the Club's Committee.

In fact, if we look at the trio's typed advertisement to publicise the first walk, to be held on Sunday 14th February 1943,[13] it indicates a fundamental reason for the formation of the CBC. Apart from detailing the route and transport arrangements etc., the flyer states:

> Hitherto, Catholics belonging to Bush Walking Clubs have found it difficult to attend Mass before making the early start specified, and weekend camping trips are out of the question for the same reason.[14]

One of the most distinguishing features which marked out Catholics in those days was attendance at Sunday Mass. Catholics interested in walking could attend their parish 6am or 7am Sunday Mass and still make the 9.30am meeting time at Central Station, platform entrance number five. As an aside, we need to keep in mind the heightened sectarianism that existed between Catholics and Protestants. Incidentally, customs die hard in the CBC. Every year since the first walk on 14th February 1943 the Club notes the anniversary by holding a special walk which over the years has had various names but is now called the President's Walk. *41*

The second walk took place on 7th March 1943. The first General Meeting was held on 11th August 1943. The first President was Paul Barnes. The first Secretary was Dorothy Clayton. Of the thirteen walks on the first programme, seven were in the Royal National Park, five on the North Shore, and one at Glenbrook.

Very soon after the first walk, the Rosary was recited on every walk. Even today, the senior members of the Club still pray the Rosary on their walks. On the suggestion of Dot Clayton, the Club adopted as its Patroness "Our Lady of the Way". Dot learnt the hymn during her time in England. The world's most famous shrine to Our Lady of the Way is in the Jesuit church, the Gesù, in Rome, under the Italian title "Madonna della strada". Dot's Jesuit parish church in Ridge Street, North Sydney, also had a shrine to Our Lady of the Way. By 1952 a shrine to Our Lady was set up in a grotto in Blue Gum Swamp Creek, Springwood. The dedication ceremony took place on Sunday 27th September 1953. This site was within the property of St Columba's College, the seminary. It was interesting that *The Catholic Weekly* commented, obviously without thinking as I am, that, 'His Eminence the Cardinal has given permission for the Shrine to be erected in a grotto on Blue Gum Swamp Creek'.[15]

It is interesting because the Cardinal, of all people, has to give his approval for a statue in a creek bed! Given the broad view, from today, such a comment is, frankly, quite silly.

By now it should be clear that this initiative was both clearly Catholic and all about bushwalking. So, when today, it sounds strange to many people's ears to hear of a Catholic bushwalking club, the reason is so that Catholics would not miss Sunday Mass and still enjoy outdoor activities. An early summary of the reasons for the Club's existence was expressed in amendments to the Constitution proposed in July 1948:

> The objects of the Club are: (a) To unite Catholic recreational walkers. (b) To encourage walking as a recreation and to give assistance, wherever possible, in regard to routes, schedules, and ways and means of appreciating and enjoying the bush. (c) to practise a regard for preservation of wild life and conservation of the bush. (d) to promote social activity among members.[16]

Dot Clayton remained in the CBC all her life. Quite early in the Club's history she was acknowledged as the force behind the Club:

> Fr Coughlan moved that in consideration of Dorothy Clayton's unique position in the Club and the fact that she is the foundress of the Club,

together with her unfailing interest and enthusiasm since the Club's inception, that she be given the status of Honorary Member.[17]

On the occasion of the Club's 50th Anniversary in 1993, Dot wrote to the President. She referred to the first walk on 14th February 1943, named those who attended and concluded:

Our Lady of the Way provided a lovely day for the 1993 event, & I pray that she will guide all C.B.C members safely to our heavenly home.[18]

She died in 2004, aged 91, and was buried from St Mary's, North Sydney. Now, back to her co-founder, Fr Coughlan, who would become a figure "larger than life" in Club history. He was held in very high esteem by many Club members and quickly received the affectionate three letter title FRC, Father Richard Coughlan.

Father Richard Coughlan

Richard Bede Coughlan was born in October 1903. His family lived next to the Josephite Convent in Rockdale. He went to Marist Brothers, Kogarah. After leaving school he worked as a clerk for the Lands Department. He studied for the priesthood at Springwood and Manly seminaries. He was ordained in St Mary's Cathedral, Sydney, on 1st December 1930, aged twenty-seven. He served as assistant priest in the parishes of Annandale and Darlinghurst. In 1942 he was appointed Bursar at St Patrick's College, Manly.[19] It was while at Manly that he got the phone call from Fr Thomas to be the spiritual director of this new Catholic club. In 1946 he was appointed Parish Priest of the new parish of Gladesville where he remained until his death on 13th July 1979, aged seventy-five. Apart from being Chaplain of the CBC from 1943 to 1963, he was Chairman of the Board of Radio Station 2SM for twenty years and a Notary, later the Defender of the Bond, in the Tribunal for Matrimonial Causes.[20]

Fr Coughlan's love of the bush started when he was in his late teens. In 1922 he walked into the Burragorang Valley from Wentworth Falls. He did many walks in the area along the Cox's River, which is all now covered by the waters of Lake Burragorang and forms the stored water for Warragamba Dam. He got to know the McMahon family. Eventually, when FRC and four of his priest friends[21] wanted to acquire a property in this area, the McMahons brokered the deal. The site selected was on Scott's Main Range, providentially higher than the current water level of the dam. The Shack, as it was named then still exists and is used regularly by Club members, was built in 1940. The hut was given the formal name 'Kiaramba', which was the name of a sub-tribe of the greater Gundungurra people of the Blue Mountains. In 1941 an ironbark chapel was built by a local man, Bert Reiner. The first mass was said on 20th September 1941. With the smells of a newly built Shack and Chapel in his nostrils, FRC penned the following in late 1941:

> The silent night in silence dies .../The sunlight pours from broken skies./ Gullies fill with liquid song/Of lyrebird and chillawong.[22]/'Tis dawn/At Kiaramba

> Through the open slabs the sunlight falls/On crucifix and chapel walls,/ Making almost equal bright/Candle stick and candle light./'Tis morn/At Kiaramba.[23]

From my point of view the following aside is very telling. FRC respected canon law, whether it was motivated by courtesy or Christian meekness it matters not. In the midst of planning and acquiring the Shack property, FRC had written to the parish priest of Burragorang, Father A. J. Hickey. The latter replied saying he welcomed FRC's adventure:

> As far as I am concerned I shall be only too pleased to co-operate in all your proposals re the semi-public oratory in the Kowmung. I understand that your property will not be resumed in the dam scheme, but I fail to see how you will have access to it except by Wentworth Falls, and that way is almost impassable. [...] I think you will have to get an aeroplane. [24]

The reference to the Kowmung is the Kowmung River which was a major river deep below the Shack property to the south-west. Notice also that by the early 1940s people were aware of the proposed Warragamba Dam and how it would affect livelihoods and families in the catchment area. Incidentally, the Sydney Catchment Authority, the current institution in charge of the Dam, is holding 50th anniversary celebrations of the opening of the Warragamba Dam in 1960 on Sunday 17th October this year, the same day as the canonisation of Mary MacKillop.

The reference to the semi-public oratory is eye-catching for the student of church law. The Congregation of Rites in Rome had declared in 1899 that in 'In these oratories, as, by the authority of the ordinary, the holy sacrifice of the Mass can be offered, so also all those present thereat can satisfy thereby the precept which obliges the faithful to hear Mass on prescribed days'.[25] In essence, the semi-public oratory was erected on private not church land in which Mass could be celebrated and the public could attend. As the Parish Priest was in charge of the celebration of the sacraments in his parish, FRC was bound to consult him and seek permission if he wanted to say Mass within the parish of Burragorang. He was also bound to seek the permission of a higher authority, the Archbishop of Sydney, Norman Thomas Gilroy, who had succeeded to the See of Sydney on 8th March 1940.[26] Eventually, this was forthcoming but it took some convincing.[27]

Another example of FRC's canonical conscience can be seen in almost the last year of his life, 1978, when he was celebrating Mass at his property known as Wooglemai (named after the explorer Barrallier's aboriginal guide), which is in the parish of The Oaks, Diocese of Wollongong. He was celebrating Sunday Mass for bushwalkers in the Wooglemai chapel. After the Creed he told the congregation that he could not give a homily because, as a priest of the Archdiocese of Sydney, he could not preach in the Diocese of Wollongong without the local Ordinary's permission. He had not sought that permission. He is reported to have said:

> With respect to those present who would like to hear a sermon, I must apologize that you will have to bear with me in ensuring that the provisions of Canon Law must be complied with. For those of you who did not particularly want to hear a sermon, no apologies are necessary.[28]

Who said canon lawyers do not have a sense of humour?

These are minor things in the overall story of the club and in the person of FRC. Many members of the club over the decades and those associated with FRC acknowledge his positive influence on their lives. He is seen as a dedicated priest, loving pastor, and man of conviction and decisiveness. He was a good listener and allowed others to put their case. In his oversight of the club on behalf of the Sydney hierarchy he could be authoritarian, strict and uncompromising. Still, there are many written testimonies about how encouraging and helpful he was to the young people of the Club. He is like the majority of priests or of anyone at all. When in a position of leadership, you attract both admiration and denigration. FRC once said:

> Whatever successes the Club has achieved, whatever benefit it has been to the Catholic community, whatever joy and happiness it has brought to individual members, is due to the fact that we have tried to apply the church's principles to our own little organization – unity in essentials; liberty in non-essentials; charity in everything.[29]

FRC was not the original author of that well-known phrase. John Wesley falsely attributed it to St Augustine. In our era, it was used by Pope John XXIII in his encyclical Ad Petri cathedram, 29th June 1959, n. 72.[30]

Lest we fall into purely romantic reminiscences or hagiography of FRC, we should call to mind some moments of crisis for the CBC in its history under the domination of its first chaplain, FRC.

Mixed Camping

When one listens to CBC folklore, you get the impression that mixed camping, boys and girls sleeping in proximity to each other – definitely not together – was often a big issue in the first twenty or so years of the Club's history under the direction of FRC. Our Club historian, Jim Barrett, gives a rather sober account of this subject in his recent book.[31] He says there was nothing in the Club's Constitution or By-Laws which prevented mixed camping. But it was not the done thing at the time as observance of Catholic moral teaching and gentlemanly behaviour was in the ascendancy. Even so, the Club's Committee had been approached by Fr Thomas as far back as early 1944 on this matter. At the Committee meeting on 11th April 1944, item 10 on camping reads:

> Fr. Thomas had approached Paul Barnes and Dorothy Clayton and said it may be against Catholic ethics to have mixed camping trips. It was resolved that the camping activities on the current programme be temporarily suspended until a decision is made by Archbishop Gilroy.[32]

I wonder if looking forward to such decisions made Archbishop Gilroy really happy and fulfilled in his role as chief shepherd of the Sydney flock. But seriously, the need to consult him proves how much in control of lay affairs the hierarchy were. A Minute of the Committee Meeting on 1st November 1944 says that any change in the Constitution had to be approved by His Grace, Archbishop Gilroy.[33] In my view, FRC himself reflects this degree of control over Club affairs in later years and even the personal lives of members as well. This is the tip of the iceberg about a topic that can be seen in many other aspects of Catholic lay life in these post-war years.

The mixed camping discussion in the Minutes of 1944 to 1945 revealed much about members' attitudes, compliance with what Fr Thomas called 'Catholic ethics' and hierarchical control. The Minutes of the Committee Meeting of 9th May 1944 contain the following item:

> Fr Thomas suggested [via telephone call with President Paul Barnes] we hold a round table conference on the camping question, members of the committee to meet Frs Thomas & Coughlan. Marj. Pollard, Paul Barnes & Joe Lyons chosen for this meeting.[34]

The round table conference went ahead. A brief report appeared in the

Minutes of the Committee Meeting of 8th August 1944:

> On Tuesday, 1st August, Marjorie Pollard, Dorothy Clayton and Paul Barnes attended a conference with Frs Thomas and Coughlan. The subject discussed was mixed camping. It has been decided that the Club should not conduct official mixed camping trips. It was further decided that nothing relative to this rule should appear in the Constitution or the rules. [...] It was mentioned that in the near future a Chaplain would probably be appointed, & he could then exercise his discretion in particular circumstances as to whether any trip could be conducted.*35*

So, we have here an unwritten law which can be enforced or dispensed at any time. Ah, the beauty of church law! Note the use of the word 'Chaplain' and not 'Spiritual Director', as the title later came to be widely used.

From the early years a number of girls wished to tackle the harder walks which it was thought were the province of the boys. They proved themselves without too much opposition from the boys and the big boy himself, FRC. Some of these hard walks required overnight stays in the Blue Mountains due to the early starts the next day. Some involved a whole weekend. Where were the girls to sleep? On one occasion some CBC girls arrived at the camping cave at Kanangra Walls quite late. They bedded down in this dank, dark and large overhang. When they woke the next morning they found they had slept next to some boys whom they did not recognise. One girl is supposed to have said that she did not break the mixed camping rule because the boys were Protestants!

According to the Minutes, nothing was mentioned between 1944 and 1951 on the subjects of mixed camping or girls' camps. However, there exists a circular written on 22nd June 1945 by club President Paul H. Barnes. It advises that an Extraordinary General Meeting will be held on 27th June to 'discuss an urgent matter of importance to every active member, and vital to the very existence of the Club'.[36] It appears this was Paul Barnes's rearguard action in favour of mixed camping in opposition to the hierarchy's view. We can easily guess who won. I can find no document which shows that it was this issue which led to Paul Barnes's resignation from the Club. However, it is club folklore that Paul Barnes and about eight of his companions resigned because they opposed the ruling on no mixed camping. This folklore is not to be dismissed as wishful thinking. My point is that there is no documentation to prove it.

As the very fit and keen girl walkers were beginning to make their prowess known, the following minute appears for January 1951:

The question of Camp Trip for girls was raised & after much discussion, it was decided to put such a Camp Trip on the next programme.[37]

On another occasion, four members walked into *The Shack* on a June weekend in 1954. FRC was in residence on holidays. He welcomed them warmly and, in keeping with tradition, offered them a rum toddy to finish off the evening around the fire. It had been suggested that the only girl in the group sleep in the chapel, quite separate from the shack. This would observe propriety. As the evening came to a cheery end, it appeared to all, including FRC, that it was unfair to banish the girl to the cold chapel. All four walkers slept on the Shack floor in front of the fire. Following a few more similar incidents, FRC announced at a General Meeting that the restrictions on mixed camping were suspended for a period of twelve months before a review. According to Jim Barrett, 'No further pronouncements were made on the subject'.[38] In fact, that General Meeting was held mid-year 1955. The Minutes of the Committee meeting of 4th May 1955 mention mixed camping:

> Father Coughlan reported having interviewed His Eminence Cardinal Gilroy last Tuesday and when it was explained to him that the age group of the Club was now much higher than it was 10 years ago he relaxed the rule which he gave forbidding mixed parties on week-end walks with the requirement that the matter be reviewed after 12 months.[39]

It is quite likely that the meeting between FRC and the Cardinal never took place. If it did, FRC would not have interviewed the Cardinal, rather the other way around. But the most obvious question is what real difference does age make? The fact is that the ban on mixed camping had become unworkable. Girls were proving to be stronger and in some cases better walkers than the boys. The Grade 1 female walkers were in some cases strong personalities – they still are today. While they were all very respectful to FRC, he would have taken the point. A judicious outcome for all – it's a pity it did not happen years before.

1960s to 1980s

This era in the Club's history was one of great expansion. Here I am speaking about the large increase in membership into the hundreds. The expression of Catholic faith amongst the members was paramount. The devotional practices of the Club were front and centre. These included the praying of the Rosary on all walks; the annual Mass and Communion; annual visit to the Shrine of Our Lady of the Way at Springwood; a walk to four churches within the metropolitan area; an annual deceased members mass; and other devotional practices. Some of these devotions continue today if in another form or place.

The growing confidence of members in bushwalking meant turning their adventurous spirits to New Zealand, Tasmania, Victoria and elsewhere. Activities such as caving, rock climbing, and canyoning became popular. I was on a trip in south-west Tasmania about ten years ago with a group of club members when the eldest declared (Frank Simons, then aged 66) that he walked the Arthur Plains in 1954 when there were no maps and no mud. I embodied the spirit of the club by declaring that 1954 was the year of my birth!

It was sadly inevitable that with the widening of horizons and the more adventurous exploits came some deaths of members as a result of accidents. The first occurred in the 1955 with the death of twenty something Frank Cooper on Mt Cook in New Zealand, and Jack Murphy in Glenbrook Gorge in the same year. The last was Paul Bell a couple of years ago as he was abseiling on Boars Head near Katoomba. Fortunately, there have been very few fatalities compared to the number of adventures undertaken and the numbers who have walked over the last sixty-seven and a half years.

One of the early, and unstated, wishes of those in charge of the club was that good Catholic boys would marry good Catholic girls. This is exactly what happened. Our club historian, Jim Barrett, has done the statistics for us. In Chapter One of *Through the Years*, there is a photograph of three generations of Catholic Bushwalkers. Jim Barrett makes the point that 'all of the 3rd generation children in the photo (except one) have become members of the Club.'[40]

For all the self-congratulating, Jim Barrett also points out that the decade of the 1960s also witnessed much rancour amongst club members. In the wider context of the world, such dissensions, politicking, rivalry and bitterness is attendant on any human endeavour where joint purpose and action is on display. When looked at historically through the lens of Christian meekness such behaviour is contrary to the gospel and the New Testament. But it still happens, even amongst the highly motivated.

Admittance of non-Catholics

The St Francis of Assisi Catholic Ramblers Club (England) constitution states that the object of the Club shall be to promote friendship among Catholics chiefly by means of rambling. The Club programme frequently stated 'your Catholic friends will be very welcome'. The first Club magazine

(December 1948) carried a note from the Secretary saying 'non-Catholics are not permitted to be introduced on any occasion whatsoever into any Club activity'. Catholics conscious of the prejudice against them preferred the company of those who shared their faith and joined the Club because it was a Catholic club. Rambles started later than in other clubs to allow time to go to Mass first.

Members began wanting their non-Catholic fiances and friends to be able to join. Also Catholics, in general, were becoming more ecumenically minded. There were lively debates at the Annual General Meetings. It was argued that, as happened elsewhere, the club could cease to be Catholic and being the same as any other rambling club there would be no point in belonging to it in preference to a local club.

In 1983 a motion was carried allowing non-Catholic relatives or friends of existing members to become associate members. Only full members could serve on the committee. The Club constitution remained unchanged. Ironically non-Catholic associate members probably find it difficult to attend their own services now that rambles can have an early start because of vigil and Sunday evening Mass.[41]

It appears the English equivalent was more enlightened than ourselves. From its earliest days, the CBC Constitution made it clear that the club was for Catholics only. Our anguished years on this matter, the admittance of non-Catholics to the club, were during the 1990s. The proposal was not to make them full members but simply Associate members. The Spiritual Director, Fr Frank Bendeich, wrote to Cardinal Clancy on 20th June 1992 seeking his view on the matter. The Cardinal replied on 27th June, 'I have no problem about the matter running "its natural course" '.[42]

The proposal was put in the form of a motion at a General Meeting of the club on Wednesday 22nd July 1992. The proposed change to the Constitution was circulated to all members on 21st October 1992.

I have just said these were times of anguish. That is not too strong a word. Without going into details at this stage, this controversy signalled clearly what had long been the case, though understated. The Sydney hierarchy no longer had control over Club affairs. This was a great contrast to the days of FRC. Cardinal Clancy had given his tacit approval to the proposal.

Yet, this was not sufficient for the loud and vigorous opposition to follow his ruling, as would have been the case decades before. Even the teachings of such an august body as an Oecumenical Council, Vatican II (1962 -1965), would not sway the opposition. Some members of the opposition would protest their orthodoxy and loyalty to the Church. Yet in this matter they appeared utterly blinded. The fallout led to some members resigning from the Club in protest when the motion to admit non-Catholics was narrowly passed. The attendance at this meeting was a record for the Club, almost a third of the then membership which was about 300 people. The fallout also hastened the decision of the then Spiritual Director, Fr Frank Bendeich, to end his term on 26th September 1998 after twenty-four and a half years of selfless service. His resignation was graciously accepted by Cardinal Clancy. The full story has yet to be told.

End notes

1   Jim Barrett, Catholic Bushwalking Club Inc., 2008.
2   The Catholic Weekly, July 1979
3   Melissa Harper, UNSW Press, Sydney, 2007
4   Dorothy Clayton, *Circular*, 31.7.43, CBC Archives.
5   The Catholic Women's Association was established in 1913. It was renamed the Legion of Catholic Women in 1941 and in 1959 the Catholic Women's League. Its aim was to provide Catholic women of Sydney with a broader society, one which crossed parish boundaries and provided them with a focus for social life. For many years the CBC met in Legion House, Castlereagh Street, Sydney.
6   *The Catholic Weekly*, 12th February 1953.
7   Jim Barrett, *Through the Years with the Catholic Bushwalking Club*, CBC, 2008, p 53.
8   CBC Minutes, Book 2, 3.10.45 to 8.6.49, p 127A.
9   The title changed when Fr Peter Blayney, appointed as Chaplain to the Club in 2003, replaced the outmoded title with the more appropriate "chaplain".
10 Barrett, *Through the Years*, p 53.
11 CBC Minutes, Book 1, 13.10.43 to 5.9.45, item 17, p. 24
12 Dorothy Clayton, 'How It Began', in *The Catholic Bushwalker*, Tenth Anniversary of the Foundation of the Club, Sydney, 1953, p 10.
13 Four people (Paul Barnes, Rhonda O'Dea, Bryan O'Dea, Dorothy Clayton) completed this walk on a very hot Sydney day. The route: Mt Ku-ring-gai – Calna Creek – Berowra Creek – Hornsby.
14 Ibid., p. 51.
15 12th February 1953.
16 CBC Minutes, Book 2, 3.10.45 to 8.6.49, p. 127A.
17 CBC Minutes, Book 3, 13.7.49 to 13.8.52, pp. 84B – 85B. This tribute could have been inspired by CBC member Reg Campion in his letter of 5.10.49 to the Secretary, Joan Delaney, CBC Archives, General Correspondence, 1949 -1952. Dot Clayton wrote to the Committee on 2.12.50 in appreciation for being made an Honorary Member. About FRC, she wrote, 'Please also thank Fr. Coughlan for the embarrassingly nice things he said about me at the meeting. [...] my appreciation of his constant enthusiasm, helpfulness, tireless energy and ready sympathy which have been apparent right from the start. I don't know what the

C.B.C. would do without him'. CBC Archives, General Correspondence 1949-1952.

18 Letter of Dot Clayton to Helen Plowman, 21.2.93, CBC Archives.

19 *Australasian Catholic Directory 1945*, St Mary's Cathedral, Sydney, p 149.

20 Ibid., p 126. The Official Year Book of the Catholic Church of Australia New Zealand and Oceania 1964-65 lists Rev. R. B. Coughlan as the Defender of the Bond, p. 94.

21 Fathers Frank McCosker, Keith Bush, Stephen Ford and Tracey Boland.

22 An early twentieth century term for the Pied Currawong.

23 CBC Archives, *FRC Walk Log*, Sheet 1941.

24 Letter of Fr A. J. Hickey to Fr Richard Coughlan, St Paulinus' Presbytery, Burragorang, 16th June 1941, in private collection.

25 23 Jan., 1899

26 Norman Gilroy was born in Sydney on 22nd January 1896; ordained priest in Rome on 24th December 1923; appointed Bishop of Port Augusta on 19th December 1934; translated to Sydney as Coadjutor Archbishop, with right of succession on 1st July 1937; succeeded to the See of Sydney on 8th March 1940 and created Cardinal Priest of the Title of the Four Crowned Martyrs on 22nd February 1946. See *Australasian Catholic Directory 1947*, St Mary's Cathedral, Sydney, p. 70.

27 Jim Barrett, *Shack Country ... And The Old Burragorang*, Guntawang Youth Centres, Sydney, 1990, p 14.

28 *The Catholic Bushwalker The Fortieth Anniversary*, Catholic Bushwalking Club, Sydney, 1983, p 19.

29 Jim Barrett, *Shack Country ... and the Old Burragorang*, Guntawang Catholic Youth Centres, 1990, p. 13.

30 One scholar says the origin of the quotation comes from the time during the fiercest dogmatic controversies and the horrors of the Thirty Years' War. This famous motto appears for the first time in Germany, A.D. 1627 and 1628, among peaceful divines of the Lutheran and German Reformed churches, and found a hearty welcome among moderate divines In England. This is how John Wesley came to use it. See Steve Perisho, http://www9.georgetown.edu/faculty/jod/augustine/quote.html.

31 Barrett, *Through the Years*, Chapter 4.

32 CBC Minutes, Book 1, 13.10.43 to 5.9.45, p. 19.

33 Ibid., item 10, p. 43.

34 Ibid., Item 6 (e) (iii), p. 22

35 Ibid., Item 12, pp. 32-33.

36 CBC Circulars 1943/60.

37 CBC Minutes, Book 3, 13.7.49 to 13.8.52, item 10 (b), p. 96B.

38 Ibid., p 58.

39 CBC Minutes, Book 4, 10.9.52 to 1.6.55, p. 155c.

40 Barrett, *Through the Years*, pp. 36, 60.

41 See http://www.stfrancisramblers.org.uk/, 113 Attitudes to non Catholics joining.

42 Letter of Cardinal Edward Bede Clancy to Fr Frank Bendeich, 27th June 1991, CBC Archives.

THE INSTITUTE OF COUNSELLING, STRATHFIELD

by David Bollen*

'Institute' – it's a heavy word, impersonal, smacking of structure and formality.

'Counselling' – a method involving professionals working with clients, experts helping the needy or troubled –all very good but remote from most of us.

You may thus not have warmed to the subject of this talk – the name is not compelling and the story behind it is little known. The Institute of Counselling, as Father Ed Campion notes, 'was a largely unnoticed lay achievement of the Vatican II church.'[1]

How many of us know something of the Institute story? Who had never heard of it before it appeared on your programme? I admit to being a one-eyed man in the kingdom of the blind – I found out about it when asked to write its history. Perhaps our ignorance is excusable. People closely connected with the Institute sometimes called it the Archdiocese's best kept secret.

Operating from 1970, the Institute's classes were first held in the parish hall at Lavender Bay with office space at Cusa House, Elizabeth Street, provided by the Catholic Family Welfare Bureau. It was a shoestring affair, dependent on the Bureau and religious orders primarily, otherwise self-financing. The Christian Brothers at St Patrick's College, Strathfield, provided a teaching place for many years. The Institute is now on the ACU campus at Strathfield with linked graduate and post-graduate courses and an enrolment of seventy or so, a well-run but not ground shaking outfit – as it has been over the last forty years.

Why take an interest in its history? One reason is that it has an extraordinarily rich archive – for this old delver, as good as, or better than, anything I've worked on. Two of the Institute's leading lights were Ron Perry and Bryan Gray, Marist Brothers. Brothers were thorough – as you will remember – and these two especially so. I doubt if there have ever

* David Bollen is an academic, historian, and author of *Up on the Hill: A History of St Patrick's College*, Goulburn (UNSW Press, 2008) which won the 2009 NSW Premier's Community and Regional History Prize. His book *Opening Up: A history of the Institute of Counselling* was published by John Garratt Publishing in 2009. This talk was given to the Australian Catholic Historical Society on 15 May 2011.

Journal of the Australian Catholic Historical Society 31/2 (2010/11), 53-59.

53

been courses offered in this country where prospective students were more closely vetted, in which course evaluations were so detailed, or analysed and reported so fully. You can almost re-live the student experience.

Seeing an educational enterprise in terms of its impact on students is interesting in itself but is made more so by the nature of the student intake, especially in the first two decades. Most were religious, Sisters, Brothers, regular priests, middle-aged to youngish people who were adapting to rapid social change and a post-Vatican II ferment. What they said of their Institute experience amounts to a spiritual biography of a generation, products of one era finding their bearings in a bewildering, hopeful world of change. The records of the Institute, in short, bring a singular generation and a crucial phase in Australian religious history into focus. More of this anon.

Perhaps you are not used to big claims being made for the Archdiocese of Sydney as pioneer or innovator. So, it may be asked, how did the Institute, an agency of the Archdiocese, always dependent on arch-episcopal favour, come about? Origins are seldom simple – the book will give you the story in some detail. But if you want a summary here it is, in dialogue form:

Bishop Muldoon said: 'We'll give you five minutes.' And I said 'That's no good to me, My Lord. I don't want five minutes. I want at least half an hour before you go away and think about it.' 'Oh certainly.'

The year is 1968; the setting is the Archdiocesan Pastoral Council, recently formed by Cardinal Gilroy in response to a Vatican II prompt, chaired by his auxiliary bishop Thomas Muldoon, parish priest of Mosman but best known as a former professor at the Manly seminary. The other party is Mary Lewis, social worker at the Family Welfare Bureau, Sydney University graduate, columnist in the Catholic Weekly, panellist on Channel 7 and much more.

What Mary got Bishop Muldoon to go away and think about was the germ of the Institute, not the Institute as such – that was still to be designed – but a course on counselling conducted by qualified persons. The Council subsequently endorsed the idea and the cardinal assented. It was perhaps the Council's only significant achievement. Gilroy had little use for an advisory body and Muldoon soon lost interest. Meanwhile Lewis and her fellow movers, on the Council, at the Family Welfare Bureau (notably Father Peter Phibbs, the director, whose social work qualification was gained under Lewis' supervision), in the wider church and in related professions, turned their minds to questions of what might work and how – the challenge of getting something acceptable under way, not too ambitious but more than a one-off course.

Constitutionally, all was to be under the Archbishop's control – he would appoint a board from persons nominated, initially by a working party of the Council and the Bureau director, then by the board. Of the nine whose names came forward six were in lay life, five had professional qualifications, three were women. Phibbs, the sole priest, was to be chairman; Sister Mary Jane Bang RSC represented Major Religious Superiors, female; Brother Victor Perry FMS was the male equivalent. Credentials, good Catholic credentials, were laid before the archbishop. No objection was raised, they looked a safe bunch though the balance was unusual – and no accident.

Something new was taking shape. Lewis and her intimates wanted a professional offering, not to train professional counsellors as such but to equip people in caring, helping roles with a counsellor's awareness and understanding. From their perspective, the church's agencies were due for review – charity and selfless labour were not enough. Many of the carers, in hospitals, homes, orphanages and schools, known to Lewis and others in the course of their work, were ill-equipped and facing troubles, personal and institutional. Professional input was needed – the core group was of one mind on this. Only one of the board members might be termed an old-agency loyalist.

Had the core group rightly read the signs of the times? It's one thing to have a good idea, and it's important to get the right instrument to implement it. But success can be a matter of circumstance, the prevailing climate. That's why sailing is a good schoolmaster; one is dependent, never in full charge. What was running in the innovators' favour?

The church at large should first be given credit. The Australian church had not been in the vanguard of Catholic thought or social witness, Sydney in particular had been less than progressive. Its Welfare Bureau drew on a Melbourne precedent, Melbourne having followed U S examples. But the Australian church had given education, in schools and colleges from the bush to the cities, top priority. There were varied motives but by the mid-twentieth century one outcome was making itself felt: a growing company of tertiary educated lay women and men and a growing Catholic presence in the professions. Hope of such upward movement had long sustained toiling nuns and brothers; university colleges, favoured by the hierarchy, were founded to produce an elite. And so in due course it happened but with perhaps unforeseen consequences.

By and large the elite did not fancy being a Praetorian guard, taking the lead in the church's old battles. They had concerns and priorities of their own, a different sense of Christian calling, interests, often related to their professional experience, for which the parish hardly provided – or even the wider church. They wanted to step outside the familiar circle of duties for loyal lay Catholics. For some such people the Institute had a power of attraction. You will meet a sample in the book. They, it is no exaggeration to say, became the Institute. But to go back to the start: the church should be given credit – these people were its sons and daughters, off-spring of a church since subject to much criticism, people of high worth, choice souls.

What else was running in the innovators' favour? Brother Victor Perry came back home after time in Rome, at Brussels where the Lumen Vitae *Institute Catéchèse de Pastorale* was linking pastoral care with counselling, and at various trail-blazing American centres of learning. This, remember, was the age of the Boeing 707; Australians were exposing themselves as never before, Christians included, to a wider world of ideas. Another Marist, Brother Ronald Fogarty (of hallowed memory), did post-doctoral studies at University of Chicago and picked up a Master's degree in counselling from Loyola University. The Catholic Church, in Australia and elsewhere, had been averse to early-twentieth century psychology and related disciplnes. As one writer has it 'In general, the clergy were horrified at the implications of Freudian theory which seemed to strike at the root of confession.'[2] The Code of Canon Law put Freud and co out of bounds:

> Teachers shall deal with the studies of mental philosophy and theology and the education of their pupils in such sciences according to the doctrine and principles of the Angelic Doctor and religiously adhere thereto.[3]

Contact with mental and behavioural sciences was closer by mid-century. Vatican II seemed to open the way for a fusion of faith and learning, of the secular and sacred:

> The institutions, laws, and modes of thinking and feeling as handed down from previous generations do not always seem to be well adapted to the contemporary state of affairs.

> Thanks to . . . the progress of the sciences, and the treasures hidden in various form of human culture, the nature of man himself is more clearly revealed and new roads to truth are opened . . .

> To promote such an exchange [between the Church and human culture], the Church requires special help . . . She must rely on those who live in the world, are versed in different institutions and specialties.[4]

The Institute thus had a brief from the highest quarter. For many of our elite, the decrees of Vatican II were a clarion call resonating with their life experience.

That was the pull; there was also a push. Remember this was the time of the Little Red School Book, of university sit-ins, of demos against the Vietnam War, of lewd musicals, drugs and – so it could seem – general mayhem. The regulated quiet of the Catholic classroom was disturbed; at St Pat's in far-off Goulburn, there was a bomb scare. A young teacher (still mostly religious), knowing only decorum, could land in Blackboard Jungle. For members of orders and for priests, there was a call to be re-made, to learn new ways of relating, to face an unacknowledged self. What was joy and relief for some was baffling and disillusioning for others. Drop-out rates, so perceived from an institutional point of view, reached unheard of levels; fresh starts in life, liberated selves, living the Christian life afresh but struggling in transition – seen from another point of view. Reducing the exit rate, caring for the leavers, helping others clarify their vocations and meet work challenges – the focus of various hopes, the Institute more easily got off the ground.

The course was first offered in 1970, a once a week evening programme of lecture–discussion session–lecture. It was oversubscribed – 120 applicants had to be pared down to 80; in the end 92 were admitted. Only seven were in lay life; the majority were religious, religious Sisters predominating. This was the pattern in the early years – religious Sisters by far the biggest group, Brothers next, a sprinkling of regular priests, fewer, it any, parish priests Thus in 1975: 42 Sisters, 22 Brothers, five priests. Various factors contributed to this uneven distribution. I'll briefly single out two.

The impact of Vatican II was greater on religious orders than on other parts of the Church. Their constitutions tied them to the past. They lived by a rule that covered dress, bearing towards others, religious duties and many other things. Now they were being called to reinvent themselves, to re-think communal life and their mission. There was a lot to overhaul and the orders took to the task with gusto. Older members of community might resent the shakeup but the baby boomers were keen to update. For them, obedience was not the be-all-and-end- all. The word got around that the Institute nourished personal growth and relationships, help in coming to terms with oneself as well as new skills, both social and professional.

Parish priests were a different case. They were more contemporary – they had cars and mixed freely in the secular world – yet were men apart, without the communal life of Sisters and Brothers yet endowed by ordination with a unique character and powers. They were less likely to be comfortable in the close-up encounters which Institute courses involved – and were sometimes observed to be so. Of course they were hard-pressed for time – but so were nuns and brothers. One could go further – but whatever the explanation the Institute was not made much use of by parish priests. (I should say there were notable exceptions.)

While the early intake was mostly female, the first panel of lecturers was mostly male; Margaret Topham, a social worker at Prince Henry Hospital, was the exception. Five of the lecturers in the first few years held positions at one or other of Sydney's universities; another was a psychiatrist in private practice. Apart from Ronald Fogarty all were lay. Soon women were amply represented. A second year course, which more than half the first years went on to do, had a more practical orientation, and drew on expertise from Social Work, a field which women had almost to themselves. So there was gender balance was achieved on the teaching side. And why not?, you ask. I remind you, this was a Catholic agency of the early 70's

Who gathered these people, lecturers and group leaders, a remarkable mix of talent and experience? And why did they take on working a night a week, sometimes at weekends, for the Institute? Was it the money – $10 an hour for lecturers? Hardly. They turned up because they welcomed this newcomer – there was nothing like it in the church, even in Sydney town (this was before people with business instincts saw possibilities in counselling). They turned up because they wanted to share their skills and experience with people who also turned up by choice, also at the end of a day's work, but keen to learn. It was that best of teaching/learning situations: the subject matter of common interest, the practitioner free of typical institutional constraints, the student ready for what was offered. Course evaluations down the years, meticulously administered, show an extraordinary high level of student satisfaction. Students and those who worked with them were sharers in a learning experience.

Who was the maestro behind all this? It was the Director, Brother Victor, already mentioned, whom we now know as Ron Perry. Ron was part of the start and a very large part of the next forty years. I can't hope to do him justice here but this stands out: he had the knack of attracting talent and keeping it on side – people from different backgrounds, with different kinds of expertise, many with church moorings but not all, some widely known, some still to make their mark, some serving for decades. A student was likely to work with a score or more of these people over two years. Few students then or since can have been so close to so much talent, experience and goodwill.

Ron could rely on an inner core of enthusiasts from the tea ladies to the office helpers (not that there was an office, or even a phone for a long time, just the boot of Ron's car) There was no lack of wise heads and big hearts – I won't name names for fear of leaving someone out (but take a look at the photos in the book). Ron had many gifts. He was shrewd, he kept the Institute out of trouble in unsettled times; he was flexible without being a wobbler – the Institute changed over the years, took in different sorts of students, adapting courses to higher education registration requirements and students' work aspirations, yet it was the same Institute, its values, methods and priorities maintained. Institutions look solid but are ever at risk. Ron was a great maintainer of the cause. But best of all he let it flourish, let a thousand flowers bloom, when a lesser person might have put control first and feared being swamped by talented, strong-minded colleagues. Finally, Ron assisted the installation of a worthy successor, Alison Turner, the present director.

I draw to a close, much unsaid. The Archdiocese can be proud of the Institute. It was not a top-down initiative but the Archdiocese let it happen and Sydney Catholics, lay and religious, men and women – particularly women – gave it life, shaped and sustained it. It has been about things of profound importance to Christians and to the institutional church: personhood and community. It has enriched the faith life as well as the personal and professional lives of some thousands of students. Its history deserves to be more widely known. A less than fulfilled relationship with its sponsor might thus benefit.

End notes

1 E. Campion, *Lecture on the life of Rosemary Goldie, Australian Catholic University*, 2010 (unpublished).

2 Bollen, *Opening Up*, 7.

3 *Opening Up*, 10.

4 'Pastoral Constitution of the Church in the Modern World: Gaudium et Spes (1965)", pars 7, 44; *Opening Up*, 41.

Mary MacKillop: A Rocky Road to Canonisation

by Sr Benedetta Bennett*

A day or two before the death of Mary MacKillop when Cardinal Moran was leaving after visiting her, he said to those around "I consider I have this day assisted at the death bed of a saint." In his Eulogy at her Requiem he expressed the hope that one day Mary MacKillop would be canonised.

Canonisation is the process by which the Holy Father declares in a definitive and solemn way that a Catholic Christian is actually in the glory of heaven, intercedes for us before the Lord and is to be publicly venerated by the whole Church.

Canonisation is a double statement – about the life of the person and also about the faith of the people who are alive at this moment. The faith and devotion of the people had been evident from the time that Mary MacKillop died – from the great numbers who came to view and touch her body and were present at her Requiem and burial. Today this same faith and devotion can be seen in the numbers visiting her tomb and praying in the Chapel, particularly those requesting her intercession because of some need.

When the present Chapel was completed Mary MacKillop's body was brought from Gore Hill Cemetery and re-interred in the Chapel on 29 January 1914 with great numbers of people filling the Chapel and spilling out into the grounds; so she was still in the minds of people.

In 1925 Mother Laurence O'Brien spoke to Mgr Cattaneo (Apostolic Delegate) who after discussion with Archbishop Michael Kelly (Archbishop of Sydney) instructed Mother Laurence on the steps to take. The Diocesan process needs to look at the life of the person, what she did, what she wrote and said and what others said and wrote about her.

So there was need for three Diocesan Processes:
1. Search for and examination of the Writings of the Candidate.

2. Examination of Witnesses

3. Examination of Grave site, Chapel, etc

1. Search for the Writings:

(i) A Decree was sent to every parish in the Archdiocese of Sydney to ask

---

* Sr Benedetta Bennett is a Sister of St Joseph. She was involved in education for many years and is now the Archivist in the Congregational Archives of the Sisters of St Joseph. This is the text of a talk to the Australian Catholic Historical Society, given at Mary MacKillop Place on 11 Sept 2011.

for anyone who had any letters or writings of Mary MacKillop to send them or authenticated copies to the Mother House at North Sydney.

(ii) This decree was printed in all the Catholic Papers in Australia.

(iii)A request was sent to every Bishop in Australia and New Zealand asking each to cooperate in the same way in his Diocese.

(iv)Mother Laurence wrote to all the communities of Sisters asking them to send in any letters, prayers or other writings they had of Mary MacKillop. Mother Laurence also asked those Sisters who had known Mary MacKillop personally to write their memories of her.

This request for Mary MacKillop's writings brought in some hundreds of letters as well as notes from Retreats Mary had given to the Sisters, Diaries and her own Spiritual Writings. Some of these letters engender much interest as because of the shortage of paper Mary often 'cross-hatched' the letter, i.e. she wrote one way and then turned the page sideways and wrote across it.

Mother Laurence had to appoint a Postulator (person to 'further' the Cause). Father Francis Xavier O'Brien S.J. was appointed and formally made the request to His Grace, Archbishop Kelly, to set up the necessary Tribunals within the Archdiocese.

After the tribunal had conducted eight sessions between 30 November 1925 and 1 March 1926 it was found that the proceedings had been invalid – the Promoter of the Faith had not been at all sessions and Sister Columbkille Browne was assisting as the Notary.

So the correct Tribunal was constituted on 9 April, 1926. A Tribunal is a little like a Law Court:

The Postulator prepares the case – a copy of which is given to all parties and witnesses

The Promoter of the Faith prepares an examination of witnesses and writings.

By Rescript Archbishop Kelly appointed Mgr Denis O'Haran the Promoter of the Faith (also known as the Devil's Advocate). His duty was to make sure that all formalities were observed, to look for weaknesses in the evidence and to put in a protest if and when he thought it necessary. Father William Keane S.J. was appointed to assist Mgr O'Haran. For the Notary the Archbishop chose the Secretary to the Apostolic Delegate, Dr. N.T Gilroy, a Priest of the Lismore Diocese.

The Process on Writings had been underway for five months when Father George O'Neill S.J. who was researching the life of Mary MacKillop to write her biography wrote to Archbishop Kelly urging the immediate abandonment of the Cause because he had witnesses whose evidence was too negative for the Cause to continue.

Archbishop Kelly, though he was willing to listen to anyone, always made up his own mind, so he decided to hear the witnesses.

It was pointed out to him that he could not call witnesses in the midst of the Process of Writings, so Archbishop Kelly cabled Rome to know if he could begin the Process of Witnesses before the Process of Writings was completed. On receiving an affirmative from Rome he announced that the Process of Writings was suspended for a time and proceeded with the investigation into the Servant of God's reputation for holiness. (This suspension came to be 25 years.) So the Tribunal for the Examination of Witnesses was set up on 27 September 1926.

2. Examination of Witnesses:

There were three classes of witnesses:

(i) Those on the Postulator's list (people who had known Mary MacKillop or had been told much about her by those who knew her)

(ii) Others recommended by the first group.

(iii) Witnesses called by the Tribunal (both for and against) who were called ex-officio. These are usually called last.

As soon as the Tribunal was formed the Archbishop called the "ex-officio" witnesses, especially the two on whose evidence Fr George O'Neill had urged the closing of the Cause. They found quite a difference in what was attributed to the witnesses and what the witnesses swore on oath. So Archbishop Kelly decided to call more "ex-officio" witnesses and then ruled that the charge brought against Mary MacKillop was false and had no basis.

The Process of Examination of witnesses then continued. Mgr O'Haran had arranged his questions under 29 headings with many sub-headings. This meant that most witnesses had to answer many questions to bring out their recollections of Mary MacKillop.

Monsignor O'Haran had been searching the Sydney Archdiocesan Archives during the Christmas vacation and discovered three documents about the Commission of Investigation in Adelaide in 1883 which Bishop Reynolds had sent to Cardinal Moran.

When the Tribunal resumed on March 9, 1929 after the Christmas vacation, Monsignor O'Haran, as Promoter of the Faith, lodged an objection to the continuation of the proceedings because of the documents he had found. Cardinal Moran had quashed the Report on the investigation and exonerated Mary MacKillop, but his report could not be found in Sydney, Adelaide or Rome. The Tribunal remained in abeyance while searches were made. Then Archbishop Kelly went on a visit to Europe. By the time the Archbishop returned and decided to suspend the Tribunal officially, Mgr O'Haran had died and the notary, Rev. N.T.Gilroy, had returned to the Lismore Diocese. Mgr Giles, the new Secretary at the Delegation, was appointed Notary for the closing session in September 1931. Archbishop Kelly suggested that they resume at Easter 1932.

Due to the ill-health and then the death of Archbishop Kelly nothing was done – the Cause was permitted to lapse.

In 1951 Father F. X. O'Brien S.J. (as Postulator) requested His Eminence Cardinal Gilroy, Archbishop of Sydney and the original notary, to re-open the Cause. Father William Keane became the Promoter of the Faith and Dr Colin McKay, the Notary.

As a matter of formality Cardinal Gilroy, through the Apostolic Delegate, Monsignor P. Marella, sent a request to Rome for a copy of Cardinal Moran's report on the 1883 Adelaide commission – the document which could not be found in 1929. This report was received by Cardinal Gilroy within 13 days.

At the same time Father Osmund Thorpe, C.P. who had been commissioned to write a new biography of Mary MacKillop found in the Adelaide Diocesan Archives the elusive documents Cardinal Moran had written to Archbishop Reynolds.

Father Osmund Thorpe C.P. was given the task of analysing documents, especially those dealing with the troubles in Adelaide and assisting the Tribunal to draw out the true facts.

With the finding of these documents The Tribunal moved on quickly. Though the Tribunal still had the evidence of the witnesses heard in the 1920s, fresh witnesses needed to be heard. There were still a few people alive who had known and/or lived with Mary MacKillop. Of special importance was the evidence of those who had nursed Mary MacKillop during her last illness.

The last witness was Sister Columbkille Browne the First Assistant, who had known Mother Mary, had been the Congregation Secretary for 25 years and could explain anything still puzzling the Tribunal. She had been the Secretary at the invalid sessions of the Tribunal.

After the hearing of evidence was completed the promoter presented documents which attested some of the principal events in Mary MacKillop's life, showed the work she did and supported or rebutted statements made in oral evidence.

Scribes were called in to make a copy of the proceedings for transmission to Rome. This was a rather large work as the Acta extended to 501 pages and the copies had to be handwritten on thick paper. The Notaries then had to check the two copies to make sure there were no errors of transcription. The copy was sent to Rome and the original sealed and placed in the Sydney Archdiocesan Archives

The third process: to prove no unlawful public veneration had been paid to Mary MacKillop, was then commenced. As in the second process witnesses were called and examined. As Mary MacKillop is buried in the Chapel, the sacristan was an important witness. After eight witnesses had given their evidence the Cardinal, officials and witnesses went to the chapel and inspected the tomb, other parts of the chapel and of the house to ensure no public veneration had been given to Mary MacKillop.

In the earlier processes the Cardinal, as judge, just guided the Process about the life of Mary MacKillop so that Rome could make a decision; in this case the Cardinal had to judge whether the laws about worship had been observed.

Then the Process was signed and sent to Rome for examination there. The Holy Office issued its Nihil Obstat to the introduction of the Cause on 19 July 1952. The decree approving Mary MacKillop's writings was issued on 2 April 1954.

Cardinal Gilroy decided that some additional processes to obtain more information and clarify any points that were not clear be held, so he opened processes in Sydney on 21 May 1959, in Brisbane in July and in Adelaide in May 1961. In Brisbane Archbishop Duhig who as a young Bishop had known Mother Mary and in Adelaide Sisters and a former lay teacher who had all known Mother Mary were called.

At this tribunal Cardinal Gilroy and Father F. X. O'Brien S.J. were again the Judge and Postulator, respectively. Father (Dr) Colin McKay became the Promoter of the Faith and Father W. E. Murray, the Notary.

The visit of Pope Paul VI to Australia in 1970 helped to bring Mary MacKillop to the minds of the Roman authorities as the Holy Father passed by the Chapel every day on his way to his appointments. Some of his meetings were in the Chapel and so he had the opportunity of praying at Mary MacKillop's tomb.

In 1972 a Positio (*Positio Super Causae Introductione*) was prepared and forwarded to the Congregation for the Causes of Saints. It contained a transcript of the additional evidence, a selection of relevant documents, a copy of the decree of approbation of Mother Mary's writings which was issued in 1954, a copy of the favourable judgements of these documents by two theological judges and many letters from prominent Australians.

On 4 January 1973 a meeting of the Sacred Congregation for the Causes of Saints was held, and on 30 January a Special Congregation of Cardinals. To the question "Should the Cause of the Beatification of the Servant of God, Mary of the Cross MacKillop, be introduced their Eminences declared that "the Cause might be introduced if the Holy Father should think fit." Pope Paul VI did think fit – he approved and confirmed the verdict of the Cardinals on 1 February.

At the Mass for Religious during the International Eucharistic Congress in Melbourne in February 1973 the Papal Legate presented this approbation and so Mary MacKillop became Venerable. The future Pope John Paul II was present as Cardinal Karol Wojtyla.

However, the Secretary indicated that a search for further documents and an historical study, especially as regards Mother Mary's relationship with the Bishops and Father Woods, should be made.

Monsignor Aldo Rebeschini, Secretary to Cardinal Knox in Rome, devoted most of his time when not on official duties to searching for documents.

The Archives of the Sacred Congregation for the Propagation of the Faith contained correspondence between the Bishops of Australia and the Holy See as that was the established avenue of communication.

The Irish College and Scots College in Rome also had valuable material in their Archives. The Irish Bishops often corresponded with the Rector of the Irish College, Monsignor Tobias Kirby. He had also befriended Mary MacKillop when she was in Rome, so had both sides of the story. Mary MacKillop had received assistance from the Rector of the Scots College when in Rome, so letters seeking advice from successive Rectors, Dr Grant and Dr Campbell were in that college archives.

About the time that Monsignor Rebeschini returned to Australia Sisters Teresita Cormack and Joan Luff went to Rome to find out what had to be done to further the Cause of Mary MacKillop. As a result of that visit Sister Elizabeth Murphy, our Congregational Leader, asked the Australian Provincial of the Jesuits, Father Davern Day, if he had any priest available to finish the research and write the required Positio. Father Paul Gardiner S.J. who had just finished his term in the Curia in Rome took up the research and writing in 1984. He worked under the direction of Father Kurt Peter Gumpel S.J. who was the Relator of the Cause. The three volumes of his work – two present the life and activity of the Servant of God, and the third one 'Informatio de Virtutibus' - were registered with the Congregation of Saints in early 1990.

From documentation which had been prepared in the 1960/70s and was available in the Archives here at Mount Street, Father Paul Gardiner S.J. wrote and presented a special Position Paper on the Miracle which had occurred in the 1960s.

On 23 June 1993 the Congregation for the Causes of Saints issued a decree of Beatification for the Venerable Servant of God, Mary of the Cross MacKillop. Father Paul Gardiner S.J. relayed this news by telephone from Rome to Sister Mary Cresp, the Congregational Leader. Pope John Paul II performed the ceremony of Beatification at Randwick Racecourse on 19 January 1995.

World Youth Day in Australia in 2007 and the visit of the Holy Father, Pope Benedict XVI, gave great impetus to the Cause as the Holy Father could see personally the devotion of people towards Blessed Mary MacKillop. Actually thousands of pilgrims visited her Tomb and many assisted at Mass in the Chapel which to respond to requests for access was open for something like 18-20 hours a day.

When the Holy Father received the gift of the bust of Blessed Mary MacKillop, on his visit to the tomb and chapel, he said: "She is smiling at me, I have to take her home".

In April 2008 Bishop Michael Malone of the Newcastle/Maitland Diocese set up the necessary Tribunal to examine the alleged cure of Kathleen Evans from terminal cancer in 1994. Doctors who had attended Kathleen were called to give evidence, friends and family were also asked about her; x-rays and medical documents, from the time of diagnosis until long after Kathleen was well, as well as current x-rays and ultrasounds were gathered and examined. After a panel of Doctors in Australia confirmed that Kathleen's cure could have no medical source, a Positio was written which included these documents and it was taken to Rome to the Congregation for the Causes of Saints by Sister Maria Casey, the vice-postulator, and Sister Sheila McCreanor.

In July of that year Sister Maria Casey accepted the position of Postulator and Father Paul Gardiner assisted as vice-Postulator. In 2009 it was decided that Sister Maria Casey RSJ should move to Rome to be available for any queries.

As you would have noticed, delays of many years do not seem to mean anything to the Congregation for the Causes of Saints so every few years when attending Major Superiors meetings in Rome our Congregational Leaders would seek an audience with the Holy Father and present him with a book showing that devotion to Mary MacKillop was alive and well and that people were still asking her intercession.

On 19 December 2009 Pope Benedict XVI issued a decree recognising Blessed Mary MacKillop's role in the healing of Kathleen Evans from lung and brain cancer.

Of course much work had to be done after the announcement and Sister Maria Casey remained in Rome to work on behalf of the Congregation.

The day of Canonisation came on 17 October 2010 in Rome with a contingent of about 5000 Australians celebrating. The ceremony was beamed live all over Australia.

References:

Australasian Catholic Record Vol 29 1952 Rev W. Keane S.J. 'The Cause of Mother Mary MacKillop'

Australasian Catholic Record Vol 68 1991 Rev P. Gardiner S.J. 'The Cause of Mother Mary of the Cross'

Archives: Sisters of St Joseph of the Sacred Heart, North Sydney

Faith and Politics – Dame Enid Lyons

by Anne Henderson*

Remember when we used to sing "Faith of Our Fathers". And how we never thought of it as rather narrow minded. But we should have also been singing "Faith of our Mothers". Mothers, more often than fathers, kept the faith.

It is one of those mothers I want to talk about today.

Enid Muriel Lyons was Australia's first woman to win a seat in the House of Representatives – she did this in 1943 as a conservative candidate for the United Australia Party, the party her late husband and former prime minister Joseph Lyons had helped to found in 1931.

She also won against the political tide – at the 1943 election, Labor prime minister John Curtin recorded a landslide win. Enid Lyons needed a week of preference counting before she was declared the new Member for Darwin (now Braddon, in north-west Tasmania) in 1943, which she had contested standing against six other candidates, two from her own party.

It was a remarkable achievement on several counts.

As Enid Lyons put it later about the election: "I was a Catholic and that was a point not in favour there."

This was another era, when the Protestant-Catholic divide dominated Australian politics. Enid Lyons had ridden the heights of popular appeal beside her husband Joe Lyons through the 1930s. But Lyons, as a political figure, was something of an aberration. And, after his death in 1939, Lyons' conservative United Australia Party had declined while seeing the return of much of the Catholic vote to Labor.

In addition, Enid Lyons faced huge hurdles as a political candidate, both for being a woman and the Catholic mother of eleven.

The Lyons phenomenon

The political phenomenon that was Joseph and Enid Lyons has been largely forgotten in Australia. Edmund Campion doesn't mention them in his *Australian Catholics*.

One wants to ask in all this if Joe and Enid Lyons failed to fit some sort of code for Australian Catholics in some way? It's possible. For there was

* Anne Henderson is Deputy Director of The Sydney Institute, editor, writer of newspaper articles and former teacher. She is the author of *Enid Lyons: Leading Lady to a Nation* (Pluto Press, 2008) and *Joseph Lyons: The People's Prime Minister* (New South Publishing, 2011). This talk was given to the Australian Catholic Historical Society on 17 July 2011.

nothing lacking in their Catholic faith, or political achievements.

To my mind, it's all about tribe. Australian Catholicism a century and less ago was all about tribe – a tribe under siege and on the fringes. A tribe held together by its Irish heritage and a tribe made strong by the concerted campaign of its bishops and religious orders to build a Catholic education system in the face of the secular and government system introduced in the Australian colonies in the latter half of the nineteenth century. Even Australia's first saint – Mary MacKillop – was driven by this tribal urge.

The Lyons couple stood outside the tent in much of their political life. In spite of being the most devoted practising Catholics and an example to the wider community in their very much outsiders' religious faith

Joe and Enid Lyons not only left Labor in 1931, they also joined the heavily Protestant and Masonic conservative side of politics. And Labor took a decade to recover. Catholic historians of the past half century seem to have deemed them to belong outside the tribe.

Some background

As prime minister from January 1932 till 7 April 1939 (when he died in office), Joe Lyons still matches only Bob Hawke in popularity as a PM. His win at the December 1931 election remains the record, in spite of Malcolm Fraser in 1975, for the percentage of House of Representatives seats won by any coalition of forces in the history of Australian federation.

Unlike Hawke, however, Lyons was a people's PM leading a loose force of political groups combining former Labor and conservative supporters.

Lyons, a senior minister in the Scullin Government after 1929, abandoned Labor over financial policy in March 1931, leaving first the Cabinet and soon after voting against Labor treasurer Ted Theodore's bill to print money for employment relief. Lyons was joined by five Labor colleagues. All were immediately outside the caucus.

So Lyons was a Labor "rat" and would never be celebrated as one of its heroes – in spite of his being a Labor man all his adult life until that point, a Labor MP in Tasmania from 1909 and a Tasmanian Labor premier from 1923-28.

Enid Lyons had married Joe Lyons in April 1915. He was then Tasmanian Treasurer and Minister responsible for education and railways. Until just before her marriage, Enid Burnell had been a trainee teacher. She was still 17 as she married. Lyons was 35.

Regardless of the 12 children they produced, Joe and Enid Lyons' lives together would be enmeshed in politics. Enid soon joined her husband at state Labor Party conferences and handled a lot of the paperwork in his electorate as the years went by.

Enid Lyons also often partnered her husband on stage; as a child she had entered elocution competitions with the Methodist church and acted in local productions. At a podium, she proved to be a natural thespian. She could draw out people's emotions while also making her points succinctly. Lyons, on the other hand, was a master at arguing complex cases in words ordinary people could follow. They made a great team.

Moreover, the Lyons union crossed quite significant social divides.

Joe Lyons came from Irish immigrant stock. The Lyons family of the Stanley district of northern Tasmania was Catholic in a state that was more Protestant than most. Enid Lyons, on the other hand, had been brought up a Methodist – her mother Eliza attended church and was involved in church activities while Enid's father William was a non-believer.

Strangely, it would be politics and the Labor Party that brought the couple together. Enid's mother, Eliza Burnell, was an early member of the Tasmanian Workers Political League. Here, she befriended Joe Lyons as a fledgling Labor MP. She introduced her daughters to her Labor MP friends on a visit to parliament in Hobart in 1912. Enid had just turned 15. Two years later, Joe Lyons and Enid Lyons were engaged.

It was Eliza, not Joe, who urged Enid to consider instruction in the Catholic faith. Eliza Burnell's marriage was not a happy one and she believed that difference of religion or lack of it in one partner was a poor foundation for a long-term relationship. Joe Lyons, smitten by his fresh, pretty young fiancee, said he would marry Enid if she was a little heathen.

But, as Enid reflected on the differences of faith between them – and on the Catholic Church's new teaching that a Catholic could not marry in a non-Catholic church - she was persuaded to take some instruction in the Catholic faith.

Enid's decision showed not only the place religion played in many middle class homes at the time, but also a sense of faith in Enid herself - for one so young.

Enid Burnell spent a couple of weeks at the Catholic presbytery in Stanley with her mother in early 1915. This was the parish of Joe Lyons' friend Father Tom O'Donnell. But when O'Donnell was called away to his sick sister in Victoria, it was Eliza who proved the dominant personality in the conversion. Eliza pulled books from the shelves and made Enid read them. Enid came to a belief in the Catholic tradition as the true one. The pope would have been very proud of Enid, indeed even of Methodist Eliza who had done the instruction...

Enid Lyons would record that her conversion to the Catholic faith was absolute. If her engagement had been broken she would not have returned to her Methodist beliefs. She also recorded how her engagement to Joe Lyons cost her many friends; she had no pre wedding parties as her predominantly non-Catholic friends disapproved of her Catholic fiancé. Her local minister tried to persuade her not to go ahead with her conversion. She had been one of his Sunday school teachers and she was abandoning her church.

That old time religion

Enid Lyons' faith had many trimmings. Converting to the Church of Rome, albeit one infused with Irish sentiment and tradition Down Under, she entered a tribe taking its commands from its bishops. Further, its religious ceremonies were soaked in the Latin of decades. And it was very much male dominated. Enid accepted all this unquestioningly.

However, like Joe Lyons, Enid would never become involved in the extra curricular political activities of Australian Catholic sub groups and the hierarchy. Joe Lyons did not support groups agitating for state aid for Catholic schools. He belonged, as did Enid, to the Australian Labor Party which in its early years believed it could not afford to be infiltrated by groups seeking to use it for sectional interests. The party banned its adherents from membership of such groups as the Catholic Federation.

As a UAP and Liberal Party MP, Enid Lyons did not allow herself to become any sort of mouthpiece for B A Santamaria. In the 1940s she was very friendly with Paul McGuire, who had dealings with Santamaria. But she resisted McGuire's requests to pressure her Liberal colleagues in any way.

In December 1949, shortly after Menzies had won back government against Labor, McGuire wrote asking if she would prevail on Robert Menzies to "consolidate the Catholic electors who went over at the election .... [because] a strong backing of Catholic opinion is essential if a serious move against the Communists is made" Enid replied that she could not help as she was, in her view, "very small potatoes here".

The role faith played in Enid Lyons' politics was strictly of a personal kind. She quite frequently spiced her speeches with reference to her faith and belief in God.

Campaigning as a Labor candidate for the state seat of Denison (Hobart) in 1925 she urged upon her audiences the dignity of a worker's labour, making reference to Jesus as the "central figure in all history".

The name Enid Lyons went hand-in-hand with a recognition that she was a woman of faith. And a presence in public firmly rooted in her Christian beliefs. When asked to appear on American Ed Burrows' radio series "This I believe" in April 1954, the ABC's Richard Boyer encouraged her to do so, writing: "Give 'em your fundamentals of faith in the meaning of life. Very few are able to do this or, if able, not willing to do so."

As a Catholic, Enid Lyons remained in part a traditional Methodist. That old time religion of Moody and Sankey hymns and gospel music never left her. She was a member of the ABC Board for more than 10 years from 1951. ABC historian Ken Inglis has recorded how Enid and ABC Board colleague Richard Boyer would break out in "revivalist hymns from their Methodist childhoods".

Enid Lyons was no concert pianist but she played all her life for sing songs around pianos and at church on Sundays. I was amused to find, in a file of Enid's music, a small piece of notepaper with the letterhead of the Prime Minister's residence across which she had scrawled "hymn to the Little Flower"

Keeping faith

Enid Lyons' faith crossed boundaries; it was a faith she expressed in her language, her speeches and her music. It was also a conservative faith in keeping with the church teachings of her day. With Joe Lyons, Enid expressed solidarity with those less fortunate. Against prevailing notions of economy, she spoke up in the party room for child endowment and even persuaded Robert Menzies, around the time of the 1946 election, that the Liberal Party should have a policy favouring child endowment.

As a Tasmanian MP, speaking up for the "little" man came easily to Enid Lyons – from potato farmers to widows. Her natural affinity in parliament was with members of the Country Party, in particular Larry Anthony – Doug Anthony's father. These MPs represented rural electorates like Enid Lyons' electorate of Darwin, where many electors faced problems of remoteness, precarious and fluctuating markets and the costs of distance.

As a professional – even as her husband at times faced sudden loss of income - the Lyons faith was always to trust in their personal talents – a sort of "God will provide". Even as she faced widowhood, after April 1939, Enid Lyons believed she could manage on her own with broadcasting and writing.

While she got along extremely well with Robert Menzies as a leader,

Enid Lyons' instincts did not favour Menzies' rather patriarchal airs. In her second volume of memoirs, *Among the Carrion Crows*, Enid Lyons clashed with Menzies when she recorded her reactions to his speech to the Constitutional Association in October 1938. In that speech, Menzies had criticised Australian political leaders for their weakness in the face of worsening events in Europe.

Enid Lyons regarded Menzies' comments as a direct hit at her husband. Menzies himself had reported back after visiting Germany in mid 1938 that Hitler was not a problem. Menzies' resignation from the Lyons ministry in March 1939, the day Hitler finally tore up the Munich agreement and invaded Czechoslovakia, came just weeks before Lyons died – adding to the pressures Lyons had to deal with.

In 1973, asked to give the Silver Jubilee Sir John Morris Memorial lecture – a lecture set up to honour the founding of the Tasmanian Adult Education Board – Enid Lyons delivered an address on the key principles that had guided her in life. She called her speech "The Role of the Christian Moralist in Present Day Australia".

The Australia that she then saw was one of diminishing Christian values and public figures ready to defend such values. In general, there was nothing extraordinary in apathy about the wider public good: "only a relatively few in any society seek the general good rather than their own personal welfare," she reflected. But it was an apathy in leadership that troubled her.

In a democratic society, the fundamental was the morality of human dignity, she argued. But while she agreed that "the few may not coerce the many", there was a "common right" for any minority to proclaim its views and press its arguments "in the face of overwhelming numbers". Enid Lyons had come to the end of her life and was witnessing her Christian faith – which had been mainstream when she was a child – now a diminishing reality among the signposts of public morality.

Few in Australia in 1973, she professed, were "pressing for the Christian ethic". As Enid put it, "The danger lies not in disagreement, but in indifference; not in argument but in apathy."

For Enid Lyons, from a Christian perspective, there were many moral signposts Australians had forgotten by 1973. The debt Australia owed Papua New Guinea for its part in saving Australia in World War II was one, any real attempt to make the many non-Anglo settlers streaming into Australia feel at home was another. Along with a failure to solve the dilemma over race and Indigenous Australians, a "go-slow" ethic in the workplace, and true equality for women against the "triumphant male" culture in public and private life.

And there was more. She strongly opposed the permissive society with its growing pornography, abortion, homosexual law reform and the breakdown of family life reflected in growing divorce statistics.

But, in all of her enunciated principles for the Christian moralist, Enid Lyons believed her task was to propose and not impose. She was an advocate not a disciplinarian. Her modus operandi was persuasion not dictatorship.

Without a doubt, Enid Lyons would find today's society holds even more dilemmas for a Christian moralist. Even her own extended family – from some 50 grandchildren – would have offered occasional challenges to some of her moral codes. In many ways, we all do now – that's modernity of course.

Enid Lyons remains something of an Australian icon – even if not recognised for this by Catholic historians of a particular generation. Her moral code guided her life as truly as any. She made history as a pioneer of women's equal opportunity in government. While doing this, she raised her very large family in the shadow of the Catholic church's strict teaching against birth control. And never questioned it.

Enid Lyons' Christian values and principles were her guide always. A truly great Australian Catholic.

They Called Him Old Smoothie: John Joseph Cahill

by Peter Golding*

Just over 50 years ago, on October 23 1959, the body of the premier of New South Wales lay in state in this cathedral. Beside his coffin were members of his Cabinet, some Catholic like himself, some of other faiths and some with none, kneeling together on the hard floor, as throughout the day tens of thousands of ordinary people queued to walk quietly by to pay their last respects, many brushing tears from their eyes. It was an extraordinary spectacle. If you had been there you might have noticed the lone figure of Norman Thomas, Cardinal Gilroy, the archbishop of Sydney, deep in prayer in a secluded pew. He and Joe Cahill had been friends for a long time and had fought a few battles together especially during the great Labor Party split in the 1950s.

A couple of days before at about 2.25 in the afternoon—on Tuesday October 21— there was commotion down Macquarie Street in Parliament House. That, of course, isn't all that unusual as you would know but this time it was different. Joe Cahill, who had been premier for a record seven years had had a heart attack in the Legislative Assembly while fiercely defending his government against a no confidence motion over allegations concerning the Rural Bank's lending practices.

The next morning while chairing a party meeting he had had another attack, and the day after that, on October 22 1959, he died in the Sydney Hospital next door from a third.

On Saturday morning October 24 1959 there was a spectacle that was even more extraordinary when mourners packed the cathedral to join Cardinal Gilroy as he celebrated Joe Cahill's Requiem Mass, and hundreds who couldn't find a seat spilled over into Hyde Park, and more than 300,000 people lined Sydney streets two and three deep from the cathedral all the way to Rookwood cemetery to catch a final glimpse of the casket in which lay a man who was essentially an ordinary man like themselves. Many knelt on the damp footpath, clasping Rosary beads in their hands. The police said it was the biggest crowd ever to witness a funeral procession in Sydney.

* Peter Golding is the author of *They Called Him Old Smoothie: John Joseph Cahill* (Australian Scholarly Publishing, 2009) and *Black Jack McEwen: Political Gladiator* (Mebourne University Publishing, 1996). This is the text of his talk delivered to the Australian Catholic Historical Society at St Mary's Cathedral College on 20 June 2010.

My purpose in being here today is to tell you a little about this extraordinary ordinary man Joe Cahill.

People ask me why I chose to write Cahill's biography. My first career was as a journalist, starting at the very bottom of the pile as a message boy and eventually writing politics and then a daily column. When my newspaper closed in 1957 I moved into other fields in which I did some writing but not enough to satisfy the ink that is in my veins.

When I retired in 1990 I decided to start another career writing biographies, especially about politicians whose biographies had never been written and, in my view, deserved to be written. One was Black Jack McEwen and another was John Joseph Cahill. I published McEwen in 1996, Cahill last November.

McEwen of course was a federal politician; Cahill was a state politician. McEwen was a dedicated Country party man, Cahill was a dedicated Labor party man. McEwen was prime minister of Australia but for only 23 days, Cahill was premier of New South Wales for 2758 days. McEwen was in the Commonwealth parliament for 44 years and retired undefeated, Cahill was in the state parliament for 31 years but was out of the House for three years when he and several others lost their seats in the Lang debacle in 1932. McEwen was educated by the light of a kerosene lamp in a lean-to on a soldier settler's block. Cahill left school at 13 and educated himself at night in Workers' Educational Association classes. McEwen's father was a migrant from Armagh in Northern Ireland. His stock was Presbyterian. Cahill's father was a migrant from County Limerick in Ireland. He was a Catholic. Both were very very astute politicians and great fighters.

You could say that McEwen and Cahill had a lot in common. Certainly they were alike in one respect. Both must have had a real distaste for biographers because, as I found to my discomfort, they left behind very few personal records. As a consequence in each case the research was long, challenging and frequently frustrating.

I started work on the Cahill biography in April 2004 with, you might say, a total ignorance of the man. He had died three months before I moved from Melbourne to Sydney in 1960 and I had never met him. If you had asked me then to write down what I knew about Joe Cahill I would have been battling to cover the back of an envelope and a small one at that. The same could be said of my knowledge of New South Wales politics. So it was an intriguing learning experience. Today I think I know Joe Cahill very well indeed and what I see I like. He was a good premier and a good man.

Some people might argue that he was the state's best premier.

The book is the product of four years of research during which I interviewed as many people as I could find who knew him or were around in his time. About 60 people, most of them of course quite old. Some of them too old because four or five had died before they could read it, as I discovered when I tried to invite them to the launch.

I also discovered that some I had spoken to had memory problems. One old workmate of Joe's wasn't sure who I was when I rang him. He didn't seem to hear my mentioning the book or Joe Cahill because suddenly he broke in to ask how I came to know him. "Did I know you at Silverwater?" he asked. No, I said, I had never been there. He was obviously puzzled. It must have been in Long Bay then, he decided. I assured him, and I assure you, that it wasn't in either penitentiary.

It is a nice day so I thought it would be a novel idea for me to take you on a tour around Sydney. We will start in Redfern because that was where Joe Cahill's father Thomas first lived when he migrated from Ireland in 1882 and where Joe was born in 1891 and finished his schooling with the Patrician Brothers, aged 13. We will drive passed the old Eveleigh railway workshops where Joe got his first job sweeping floors and then as an apprentice fitter. A dozen or so fellows who worked at Eveleigh ended up in politics. They included two more who became premiers, James McGowen in 1910 and Bill McKell in 1941. McKell, of course, also became a governor-general. He also accepted a knighthood for which some of his Labor party colleagues never forgave him.

We are now on our way to Marrickville where every day the Good Samaritan nuns walked to and from their house on the site of Central Railway station to teach Joe and the other Catholic kids how to read and write. Obviously, the nuns were hardy folk. We are going to pause for a moment outside the big white church on the corner of Marrickville and Livingstone roads. That's St Brigid's where Joe and his wife Esmey Kelly were married in 1922 and his five children were baptised. It is close to the Shrubland Hall where Joe attended WEA night classes to learn debating and public speaking and he and Esmey went dancing on Saturday nights. So, incidentally, did Fred Daly and his wife, Teresa. Much later on as a kid, their son Lawrie used to walk his dog passed the Cahill's place every day. He told me that when Joe died all the school children in the area were given a holiday. "I remember:" he said, "that some of us wished a premier would die more often."

In those days Marrickville was very Irish-Catholic and very Labor, some said it was an Irish-Catholic-Labor ghetto of which St Brigid's was the epicentre. The 9 o'clock Mass every Sunday was the politicians' Mass. Afterwards, local members and hopefuls and union bosses would gather near the steps to be seen and to trade gossip and caucus and maybe assassinate a few reputations.

It is relevant for me to recall here the story told of a little old lady who, arriving late for a Marrickville Labor branch meeting, genuflected as she entered the hall, causing the meeting to erupt into a gale of laughter. "They're all the same faces," the poor flustered women protested. And it was true. Most of the people attending branch meetings could be seen also at St Brigid's on Sundays, often taking up the plate or with the Holy Name sodality. Joe Cahill was always among them.

Our next stop is not far from the church on the corner of Warren Road and Roach Street. Joe's parents bought a house there in 1912 when he was 21 and he lived there for 47 years right up till his death in 1959. It was a small two-bedroom cottage with a living room which was called a parlour and an enclosed back veranda for a sleep-out and a pocket handkerchief garden. A simple house that suited a simple family man with simple pleasures, who stood in line to be served in the local shops or to get a haircut and whose fellow shoppers and neighbours never called him anything except Joe. Why should they? He called them by their first names. If anyone wanted to contact him they just looked up J J Cahill in the phone book.

It is a wonder that Cahill ever got to be anything in life let alone a premier. He must have been a real handful when he was a young fellow. He was a rebel activist who had to join the job queues when he was sacked from the railways in the great strike of 1917 with his file marked "agitator" which meant that he was never to be re-employed. Then he had a dispute with his union, the Amalgamated Engineers, which barred him from holding office for five years. But he was never lacking in confidence. In 1917 he made his first bid for a seat in parliament, in Dulwich Hill. It was an unwinable seat and he did badly. In fact he took a serious thrashing.

It was eight years before he had another chance; in 1925 in St George a multi-member seat. His prospects of winning didn't look all that great this time either because he was one of 19 candidates, four of whom were assured of election with the other 15 having to scramble for their second preferences to be elected to the fifth seat. The poll was topped by a member named Thomas Ley who was later convicted of murder and who hated Catholics with a passion. Eventually Cahill won the fifth seat after 17 ballots. Ley conceded him a miserly two second preferences, no doubt in error.

So let's follow Joe Cahill MP into Macquarie Street. He was on his feet in the House a lot from the start, asking questions, involving himself in debates, prodding Lang to act on election promises, and giving a maiden speech that caused "the honourable members on the other side to shift uneasily in their seats." Apart from ministers his name was the most mentioned in Hansard and by the end of the session there was no one in the House who did not know it. People could see that here was a smart recruit to politics. His leader Jack Lang thought so too. When he was re-elected in 1927 he made Cahill party whip. Then in 1929 came the Wall Street crash and with it the Depression and Lang's bitter fight with the Commonwealth over finance which eventually, in 1932, cost him government and Cahill his seat and another spell of unemployment.

After a while Cahill got a job selling shoes but he was determined to win back his seat and for three years he door-knocked or spruiked on street corners or on the back of a truck for votes after work and at weekends. Not surprisingly, in 1935 he was back in parliament and that's where he stayed for another 24 years.

It was not until 1941 that Labor, under McKell who had displaced Lang, won back government and Cahill was given his first portfolio—as minister for Public Works. Later he would also be given Local Government.

Within weeks of becoming a minister he was tramping around the long-closed derelict Newcastle state dockyards which within a year under his direction had been restored and would be repairing tens of thousands of tons of war-damaged ships, and he would be touring the state arranging the construction of landing strips and military camps and bomb shelters and air raid trenches. His job also was to build schools and hospitals, houses and all other government buildings. Later he took on the task of reorganising the state's electricity supply at a time when Sydney was plagued by blackouts and power rationing. He restructured municipal government in NSW, amalgamating councils and introducing compulsory voting. He was responsible for the County of Cumberland scheme which gave Sydney its first town plan and provided for its green belt and freeways and foreshore protection. And, as the man in the advertisement says, there was more. Cahill also initiated a string of water storage projects, including the Warragamba Dam, officially opened just weeks after he died, perhaps still the largest in New South Wales and he was an advocate of and signatory to the Snowy River Hydro-electric Scheme.

These are some of Cahill's achievements. There is another which political historians, and certainly the Labor party, would view as his most significant. This was his seminal role in confronting Bob Santamaria and Doc Evatt et al to insulate the party in New South Wales in the 1950s from the worst and most destructive split in its history. That was of course after he had succeeded Jim McGirr as premier in 1952. But that is one of the many Cahill stories that are too big to be told today.

I must however find the time to tell you about Joe Cahill's election as premier because it has particular resonance for an audience such as this. For many years Cardinal Gilroy's dream was to have a Catholic university in Sydney because, as he explained, "The lack of a Catholic university leaves our education system without a head, undoes much of the good achieved in the primary and secondary schools, and deprives us of the elite Catholic laity that is the glory of the church in America. I earnestly desire to remedy this defect if that is at all possible."

The cardinal also had another reason for wanting a Catholic university. He was deeply concerned that young Catholic students were being lost to the church in the free-wheeling—some were saying "pagan"—environment in the Sydney University, then the only one in New South Wales.

During World War II Cardinal Gilroy's interest in establishing a degree-awarding Catholic institution was stimulated by a chance meeting with an American Holy Cross priest, a Father Duffy, who was stationed in Sydney as a chaplain with the United States Navy, and whose congregation had founded the Notre Dame university. Duffy put the archbishop in touch with his principals in Indiana and when the war ended Notre Dame sent people out here to look at the feasibility of establishing a campus in Sydney. In the meantime, Cardinal Gilroy made representations to the New South Wales government to bring down legislation to approve a Catholic university and, very optimistically, proceeded to purchase a tract of land for the purpose.

As you can imagine, the issue was very controversial and there was substantial opposition, especially from the Protestant churches but also from within the church itself. Despite this, state cabinet under James McGirr decided to go ahead. The Education minister who was handed what proved to be a poisoned chalice was Bob Heffron who, despite being a radical left wing Presbyterian, promised Cardinal Gilroy that he would support him.

The two stand-out candidates to succeed Jim McGirr as premier when, with some encouragement, he retired in 1952 were Heffron and Joe Cahill, and a count of heads on the eve of the Caucus election suggested that

Heffron had a comfortable majority. But, as we know, he did not win.

When Heffron arrived at his office the next morning, the day of the election, five Labor members, led by the maverick Clive Evatt, were waiting for him. They told him that unless he resiled from his promise to approve the university they would vote as a bloc against him in the leadership ballot. He refused because he had given his word and later that morning, knowing he could not win, he withdrew from the contest and presented Cahill with certain victory. I am sure the irony of the situation does not escape you.

In the little time left, let us get back into the car and drive down Macquarie Street, passed Joe's office in what is now the Intercontinental Hotel on the corner of Bridge Street, and then on to Circular Quay where we will see the overhead expressway and railway. Yes, Joe Cahill was responsible for that too—and for removing the trams from the bridge. I'm not sure he was all that chuffed that they named the freeway after him and I will refrain from dwelling on the fact that he was responsible for legalising poker machines.

Finally, we are arriving at the Sydney Opera House which most people would regard as Joe Cahill's greatest achievement and indeed, monument. It is of course nothing short of a miracle.

Joe Cahill who had never been to a symphony concert or a ballet or an opera in his life became so obsessed with Joern Utzon's concept of an opera house protruding out into Sydney Harbour on Bennelong Point that he put his reputation and career on the line against enormous opposition to achieve it. And this despite widespread belief in the community that its huge cost could not be justified and that the money should be spent on housing, schools and hospitals all of which at the time were desperately needed.

People still shake their heads over the paradox of an ordinary working man blessed with little education and without pretence to culture being responsible for what surely must be the most beautiful opera house in the world.

Having lived with Joe Cahill for the last six years, I, on the other hand, now see this as entirely understandable.

The opera house is really a tangible expression of Joe Cahill's conviction that ordinary people have a God-given right to a fair share of the good things of life. He said this in his maiden speech in parliament in 1925 and it became his article of faith throughout his life.

I would like to think that Joe Cahill's story proves that regardless of background and education anyone living in Australia who has ambition and

THE KNIGHTS OF THE SOUTHERN CROSS

by Cliff Baxter*

This is a perfect setting for a talk about history.

Just over there we have the honeyed Pyrmont sandstone of the Cathedral, the creation of William Wardell, the best Gothic architect ever to come to Australia, an English convert to Catholicism, part of the architectural recovery of the Church after centuries of repression and penal laws. The German poet, Goethe, said architecture was 'frozen music.' Our Cathedral has been called, a 'prayer in stone'.

Here, where we sit today, we have a school founded by poor Christian Brothers, who had only one shabby overcoat between them and had to climb a ladder to their meagre room. While the principal two parties in New South Wales will soon contest the State Election both with Catholic leaders we need to recall our humble origins. Jack Lang, the Big Fella, told me Sydney will never be a great city through big buildings, but through great families.

Just over there in the Crypt lie the remains of our archbishops, including Cardinal 'Jimmy' Freeman.

Jimmy was famous for his wit and brevity, I shall try to follow his example.

He told the story of a young priest who gave his first homily, and then made the mistake of asking the old parish priest what he thought of it.

Well, said the old priest, it reminded me of Heaven because it lasted an eternity, and it reminded me of God because it passed all understanding!

So I'll try not to make that mistake. Less is more.

Thank you for inviting me to talk about the history of the Knights of the Southern Cross in New South Wales.

In some ways their story is a simple one – a journey of faith – but is also complex and obscured by events inside and outside the Church.

That great American journalist, Edward R. Murrow, put it perfectly when he said:

The obscure we see eventually. The completely obvious, it seems, takes longer.

So if you find in this talk I am overlooking the completely obvious

---

* Cliff Baxter is a retired *Catholic Weekly* journalist and author of *Reach for the Stars 1919-2009: NSW Knights of the Southern Cross, Bold Men of Faith, Hope and Charity* (Connor Court, 2009). This is the text of his talk to the Australian Catholic Historical Society at St Mary's Cathedral College on 13 Mar 2011.

Journal of the Australian Catholic Historical Society 31/2 (2010/11), 83-94.

83

please raise your hand and speak up. It's corny to say that the Knights, like all parts of the Church stand at a 'crossroads' because that's been going on for two thousand years,

Someone asked me what will the Knights be like in twenty years? I said I do not know what the Church will be like then.

Certainly the support and counsel of laymen, from bottom to up, will be important as it has been in the past, albeit in a different fashion.

If the Knights of the future did nothing but follow the doctrine of reasonability amidst some of the 'take no prisoners' extremists from all religious directions then they'd be valuable. The Church is staying the same while changing, and we are part of that change.

Certainly, Knights can resist the New Barbarianism of consumerism and dishonest religious fundamentalism. Should they be 'political' ?

Of course, the Knights have acted politically – they were in the front line in the fight to obtain State Aid for Catholic Schools. At the moment many of them are taking up the cudgels against Euthanasia, and fighting discrimination against people with disabilities.

Politics, however, should not be allowed to infest the Knights, indeed any part of the Church. When it has, it has been a disaster.

In my book I deal with how brother fought brother – Sydney versus Melbourne – in the squabble over The Movement. I must say nobody emerges unscathed. In one very amusing moment Cardinal Gilroy called in the two parties and made them swap sides! The Knights joined The Movement, and the Movement joined the Knights! And we think that role reversal is a modern thing! Alas it did not stop the brawling. Even now there's not a lot of love lost between Sydney and Melbourne. Recently I met our phlegmatic cardinal, and he confessed that he had ANGLICAN FOREBEARS. He roared laughing when I told him: "The problem, Eminence, is not the Anglicans, but that you are from MELBOURNE!"

I won't go into the history of how this book came existence other than to say the fact that the Knights, with their obsession for secrecy, kept burning their records, and those that existed said very little. The financial collapse of the Knights, and their loss of the Elizabeth Street headquarters are described largely from outside the KSC.

I was amazed that the KSC State chairman, Basil Toohey, a farmer from beyond the Blue Mountains and Sister Margaret Press RSJ, were able to help me transform a real jumble into a coherent form. It's not a boring history – it's about people like you and me.

The critics of the history were not always kind – at the outset I said 'This is not an obituary !'

Catholica's Brian Coyne wrote, 'This is a beautifully written obituary.'

Another reviewer in *Annals Australasia* took me to task for lack of references. What? Carton B covered with mildew?

I thought that I'd give you a synopsis of what the book's about.

After that you can have a nap, if you like, but I am very keen to have you ask questions.

Synopsis:

In 2009 the Catholic laymen's organization, the Knights of the Southern Cross in New South Wales celebrated ninety years of existence. The Order commissioned the author to write its history. The book, *Reach for the Stars 1919-2009 NSW Knights of the Southern Cross: Bold Men of Faith, Hope and Charity*, is published by Connor Court Publishing, Victoria $29.95.

The work describes how the Knights were founded in 1919 in Sydney at a time of extreme anti-Catholic fervour and employment discrimination. This was as a result of two public polls that rejected military conscription in World War I, largely through Catholic support and the two archbishops, Daniel Mannix and Norman Gilroy. 'Catholics Need Not Apply' employment notices appeared and many of their co-religionists were discriminated against in the public service and in commercial life. This, however, created a form of solidarity unknown to our present time. The vast majority voted Labor, supported trade unions and some even supported extremists like the IWWW, the 'Wobblies', and Irish revolutionary organisations. Thus it was not surprising that the leader of the Catholic backlash was a prominent Labor politician, Patrick Minahan, a wealthy bootmaker: first in the Catholic Federation, then in The Catholic Club, later as the first chairman of the Knights of Southern Cross. In and out of Parliament Minahan, an Irish firebrand, launched a constant verbal artillery against discrimination and anti-Catholic sectarianism. The executions of the rebels in Ireland were fresh in most minds. In one outburst Minahan claimed that if conscription had been carried secret groups would have risen up and turned Australia into a republic. When a political opponent called on the government to set up a Royal Commission to investigate the conditions of women in convents Minahan told Parliament that if Catholic institutions were interfered with 'there will be a mess-up here worse than that which occurred on the plains of Flanders'. There was a serious intent, however, behind the Hibernian hyperbole.

Minahan's co-founder, Joseph Lynch, was a mild-mannered country school inspector: coincidentally, they lived in the same street in Sydney's Lewisham. Lying in Lewisham Hospital after surgery Lynch wondered, 'if that operation had not been successful what would my record have been?' and determined to set up a lay organisation of Catholic men.

While Minahan was flying the Catholic civil rights banner, Lynch was more concerned that Catholics were being turned into an ignorant underclass, lacking education and decent entertainment. They were denied good reading material and exposed to a host of agnostic literature. In his travels Lynch said he was shocked at the number of Catholics who had fallen away from the Faith through weakness, ignorance, self-interest or through reading Rationalist literature. In 1917, after a chance meeting with Father Bernard McKiernan while travelling by tram to Newcastle, where Lynch was a government school inspector, they agreed on the importance of setting up a lay organisation of Catholic men. They met frequently and by 1918 had drafted a constitution for such an organisation, to be called The Knights of the Southern Cross, to be set up in Maitland.

However his attempts to set up the movement in the country failed. Lynch then turned his attention to Sydney, but felt limited because he was in his city home only at weekends. He decided to try to get the help of the clergy but was met with a lack of interest or opposition. Similar efforts in Wollongong also failed.

Just as Lynch was thinking of throwing in the towel there was a knock on the door from his neighbour in Lewisham, Patrick Minahan, whom he had met some years before. He invited Lynch to join a new Catholic society to be called the Commercial Men's Association and handed him a copy of the skeleton constitution. Minahan had been having his own problems with the Catholic clergy but eventually Archbishop Kelly sanctioned "the establishment of a Commercial Men's Association as an offshoot of the Catholic Club". The first meeting of this Association was held on the 24th March, 1919 at the Catholic Club. The first executive was installed on 1st September, 1919 of the Knights of the Southern Cross, with Patrick Minahan as Grand Knight.

Within weeks of meeting in a room at the Catholic Club, the new Knights went out and mortgaged their homes, or took out loans, or signed over their inheritance to buy the old German Club in Elizabeth Street and turn it into their headquarters. It is impossible to see this happening in our times.

Soon they had their own library, places to hold functions with strictly moderate drinking, correspondence schools in office skills and accountancy for young Catholics, Lectures on Faith from visiting dignitaries. They were able to send out inspectors to investigate discrimination in employment. Sometimes discrimination was at a junior level and the organization corrected it but if it continued Catholics retaliated and boycotted the company's products or services.

By today's standards recruitment was nothing short of astonishing, The man responsible was one William Ross, a former amateur actor and a Catholic Action polemicist, invited by Minahan to be the first general secretary, at a salary of five pounds a week. They certainly got their money's worth from Ross, who was general secretary until 1946, when he took up immigration, a man always on the move, on first name terms with prime ministers and clergy - he was a regular visitor to 'John O'Brien' (Monsignor Patrick Hartigan) at Narrandera. The Knights gave Ross two-years' paid leave to organize the 29th Eucharistic Congress in 1928. An arrangement was made with Station 2UE to broadcast talks, music and vocal items from the Cathedral and promote the Eucharistic Congress, However nobody told Ross that the services of the radio announcer was only for a limited period. He was given notice he had to take over the air waves in thirty minutes - as always Ross rose to the occasion. He enjoyed being a radio announcer. The Vatican honoured him with the Cross of Leo for the organization of the '28 Congress. Papers found after Ross' death in 1967 disclose that he regarded the staging of the Congress as his life's triumph.

Ross even sent Australian, champion egg-laying hens, chickens to the Pope – perhaps their descendants are still clucking away in The Vatican. So successful was he in his picaresque travels, meeting people, high and low, that during the 1920s the password in the Knights was 'Do you know Bill Ross?'. I think he was the greatest 'travelling salesman' for the Catholic laity of all time. Prime Minister Billy Hughes was no admirer of anti-conscriptionist Catholics but he and Ross allied against communism. He entertained Ross in his Lindfield home and for months Hughes contacted Ross about his anti-communist plans, listening to him on his ear trumpet at lunch at David Jones.

The Knights always had a close relationship with the clergy. To this day their first chaplain, Monsignor Richard Collender, is revered and his portrait hangs in their office. Some might say it was 'pray, pay and obey', but it went much deeper.

The Knights came of age, indeed so did their Church, when they organised the 29th International Eucharistic Congress in 1928. It will be forever a diamond in their helmet. At last Catholic people could stand up in public for their Faith. At a previous Congress in London the Blessed Sacrament was banned from the streets because of Protestant objection.

Who could forget '28? they said. The Church had gone from defensive adolescence into sturdy, unapologetic adulthood in Australia.

The Knights have always objected to being regarded as 'Catholic Masons', but it must be admitted that in the early years the KSC imitated some of their practices. Initiates were led blindfolded into a dark room where there was a human skull and a candle and they promised solemnly never to disclose secrets. Members were admitted by degrees.

Records were often burned, making life difficult for future historians (such as me). The old robes are now stored in boxes, food for moths.

When I told a friend I was coming here, he said:

Whatever you do, DO NOT READ FROM THE BOOK.

Damn it, I'm going to read a couple of excerpts:

The Pope and the champion chooks

More than five hundred Knights served overseas during the Second World War. The Order gave them free membership. Back home money was short. The KSC took a sympathetic view of unfinancial members. The Order also opened its heart to some fellow Catholics – the Italian prisoners of war.

Though fascism and the corporate state was conceived in their country, most of them never had the slightest interest in war. If a German gun was not trained on them they surrendered at the first opportunity. The Germans treated them with contempt.

Australians had little animosity towards their prisoners. In the Western Desert they were surprised to find white table cloths with silverware and china on the tables of the defeated Italians, and flagons of WINE! This was not a luxury, but brought in by trucks as an essential component of the Italian art of war. Alas, the Aussie soldiers were not allowed to drink it lest it be poisoned. Aghast, they watched as the plonk was poured by their superiors into the sand.

The Italians surrendered in their thousands to the Australians. When they had their first taste of canned spaghetti they thought they were being punished, and protested to Geneva.

For Catholics, conflict with the Italians was a slight embarrassment. The Pope was an Italian. He lived in Rome and could never be accused of being a fascist. He was no enemy of the A.I.F.

When the Italian prisoners discovered Australia they loved it. Here was plenty of land. If you are an Italian what do you do with it? You grow things!

More than a few of the Italians became friends with Australian families. Some of them fell in love and later married and settled in the new country.

The love affair between Italians and Australia is comically illustrated in *They're a Weird Mob*, a popular 1957 novel by John O'Grady under the pen name "Nino Culotta". Nino meets his future wife, Kay, in a Manly cafe while trying to teach her that she cannot eat spaghetti using a spoon. He takes a job as a bricklayer's labourer to improve his English. The comedy of the novel revolves around his attempts to understand English as it was spoken in Australia, by the working classes, in the 1950s and 1960s.

Bill Ross, the ever-helpful KSC general secretary, was asked to visit the Italian POWs at Hay. He went there with Father Carroll, the parish priest, to be welcomed by the friendly Australian commandant.

He said his charges were born gardeners and spent most of their time in growing their vegetables and flowers. Our main duty was to meet the chairman of the prisoners and deliver and receive messages. During our visits the lot of the prisoners greatly improved. My last memory is seeing an Italian prisoner cultivating the presbytery garden while an Australian soldier with rifle and bayonet leisurely followed. An unexpected service for the [Papal] delegation was when I was asked to select a chicken coop of Australian hens for His Holiness at Castel Gandolfo.

Castel Gandolfo is the Pope's summer residence. It is built on land once owned by the cruel emperor Diocletian. Like the Cardinal, the Ancient Roman Emperor's legate may once have asked for champion chooks and a few eggs for the larder of his imperial master. Bad luck if he did not get them. The Pope did not need any coercion to get his egg-layers.

Anti-Catholics would have loved it had they learned of Bill's chicken search for the Beast of Rome.

One problem: Bill, our hero, knew diddly-squat, zero, zilch about hens and their egg laying abilities - so he went with Monsignor King and the Papal Delegate to the Hawkesbury Agricultural College.

After consulting the experts, Ross chose a chicken coop of Australorps, a breed of hen derived from the Australian Orpington. The Australorp has a big, bold black eye, a glossy black plumage with a rich beetle-green sheen, and is a magnificent egg layer.

His Holiness was pleased with the selection, and later in the year of arrival the coop of New South Wales hens won an Italian egg laying competition.

So there is a part of the Papal Household that may be forever Aussie.

Perhaps an "Orpie" reneged on egg laying, and graced the Papal table.

R.I.P. Orpie.

An "Orpie".

During the Depression of the 1930s, the Order established an Employment Committee, placing thousands of Catholics in jobs. World war was hot on the heels of the economic downturn. The optimism of the Twenties had vanished.

More than five hundred KSC members served in World War II. Their subscriptions were paid for them while they were overseas. When they came home the KSC Employment Committee helped them find jobs. The Knights were also very active in postwar Immigration.

NSW Catholics and Knights were at the front in the 1942 Battle of El Alamein when the German general Erwin Rommel was defeated in North Africa and the tide of war turned for the first time.

Others were there when Australians repelled the attack by Japanese marines on their base at Milne Bay on the eastern tip of New Guinea. They inflicted on the Japanese their first undoubted defeat on land.

Dr Bob McInerney, now a retired Knight, gynaecologist and obstetrician, said: "The New Guinea campaign was kill or be killed – no quarter." He operated to save wounded men while bullets whizzed overhead, and sat all night with dying men of all religious persuasions or none.

Stan Arneil, who survived the concentration camps to become a credit union pioneer and an historian, said: "No one ever died alone - they were surrounded by love and prayers."

The late City KSC chairman Alex Holst recalled climbing up into his gun turret on the Lancaster bomber only to find, to his horror, that the pilot had revved up the engine, let go the brakes and was hurtling down the runway headed for Germany.

"I just hung on by my fingertips and prayed," recalled Alex.

After a Hail Mary and an Our Father he was able to pull himself into the plane and cock his gun ready for the German night fighters.

The comradeship and closeness of death gave many Knights of the Southern Cross great solidarity when they returned home.

They were also highly organized due to their military experience.

John Fletcher KSC, of Pymble, recalls that many Australians flying with RAF Bomber Command wore or carried good luck charms. His rear gunner, who was proud of his Scots ancestry, wore a tartan scarf.

"I carried always, and used frequently, a very compact set of Rosary beads in a leather pouch purchased at the stall outside St Patrick's Cathedral in San Francisco on the way to Europe on New Year's Eve 1943," said John.

He and his mates saw many Allied planes shot down after being coned by a blue light master beam searchlight. Few planes escaped after being caught in the "cone".

The crew agreed that if caught in the light, the skipper would put the plane into a spiral dive, and the navigator, a husky wheat and wool lumper from Gulgong, would leap forward to help pull the plane out of the dive when it had escaped the light.

Over Potsdam, after dropping its bombs from 20,000 feet, the Lancaster bomber, "C Charlie", was caught in the "cone" and the pilot threw the plane into a dive.

"As the Nav moved forward, he drawled, 'Fletch, get those Beads out!' to which my somewhat quicker response was, 'George, I'm already through the first decade'."

The pilot and the navigator "in a joint effort bordering on the miraculous" pulled the plane out of the dive at 500 feet with the air speed indicator off the clock at more than 400 m.p.h. - twice the normal cruising speed.

"On future missions the Nav, not an overly religious chap, asked, not in jest, 'Have you got those Beads, Fletch?'. "

"I still use that same set of Rosary beads in thanksgiving for the wonderful life that Our Lord has gifted me with my loving wife and family.

"I held up that same set of beads as I gave the funeral eulogy for that excellent navigator after he had a heart attack while cleaning out a dam on his property."

The Knights were very immigration-aware. Some of their ancestors had been among the 160,000 shipped out to Australia as convicts, or the survivors of the Irish Famine, or the hundreds of Irish Catholic orphan girls brought out as servants. They sympathized with the millions of people displaced by war in Europe.

When the Commonwealth Immigration Scheme was launched in 1945 the Knights' committee was in the box seat.

Five years after the end of World War II almost 200,000 migrants had arrived.

Ross, in his anecdotes of the postwar immigration, recalls meeting a tall man from the Bathurst migrant hostel. He was dressed in ill-fitting clothes and was working as a waiter. He asked Ross if he could persuade the Department to let him and his wife stay in Sydney so that he could visit the ABC broadcasting office. Ross phoned them and they agreed. It was Tibor Paul, the famous conductor.

Much later Ross attended one of his concerts at the Albert Hall in Canberra. He met him at interval:

Tibor Paul would not stop thanking me. That's why the interval was so long.

36

The miracle of Boronia Drive

When a new Catholic church opened in Canberra in the Seventies the parishioners wondered how it could ever be paid for. They were told: "God will provide."

The priest kept a poker face because he knew that He had already, with a stroke of good fortune and some assistance by Knights of the Southern Cross.

The Knights have always been good fund-raisers, but who would have thought they could pay off a church in a day?

In the 1970s they ran Bingo games in support of the building of St Joseph's Church in Boronia Drive, O'Connor, Canberra.

It was the good "sixty-six, clickety-click", and the money rolled in, but only slowly.

The spare change, the "shrapnel" from ticket sales, was thrown into a cardboard box.

Bert Hobbs KSC and his mates had to decide what to do with the leftovers.

They decided to buy an Opera House lottery ticket.

Wait for it. It won $200,000.

This would probably be $1.3 million in today's terms.

St Joseph's opened and was dedicated in 1973 debt-free. When they heard the news that they had a church for free, the parishioners were open-mouthed, gob-smacked, stunned. Nobody had ever heard of such a thing.

The church burned down on the Feast of Mary MacKillop on August 8, 2007, but Fortune had not deserted St Joseph's parish. Insurance covered its restoration at a cost of more than $2 million. Precious items were not destroyed by the fire.

"The wonderful stained glass windows by Harry Clarke from Dublin and the altar carvings by Polish artist Jozef Steliga were saved," said parish priest Father William Kennedy.

The church reopened on March 19, 2009.

"Nobody will ever forget the day the Knights won the lottery," said Father Kennedy.

Bert Hobbs died in 2008 aged ninety-seven.

Bill Ross certainly had the gift of the gab. P.J. Minahan chose the right man in 1920. He was a real all-rounder: much of his success he attributed to his training as a teenage debater with Catholic Action at St Charles Debating Society at Waverley.

As a young man he spoke in a contest held in the School of Arts Hall in Pitt Street. The Catholic team was opposed by "champions of the day" led by T.J. Ley, later a Liberal Minister. The young Catholic did not know it, but he was debating with a future murderer. Ross recalled:

When I was asked to speak I started eagerly. Then to my horror I went out of matter with two minutes still to go. In a panic I spoke to the Adjudicator, Mr M.D. Watt, a leading barrister of his day. "Mr Adjudicator," I said, "I ran out of matter, and I must sit down." How I dreaded his summing up and his verdict. When he spoke I was the first he mentioned. "I give high marks to Mr Ross," he said. "When he had nothing to say he had the good sense to sit down."

Ley rose to be New South Wales Attorney General as a strong Protestant temperance leader. He was known as Lemonade Ley. He stood on a prohibition platform, with a local brewer of beer funding him. He was the ultimate hypocrite.

Ley tried to bribe a Labor MP to stand aside so that he could enter federal politics. When the man refused he "went missing", presumed murdered.

He raised money to produce herbicides against the pest prickly pear - and spent all of the money on a holiday with his mistress.

When one of Ley's backers squealed he was found dead beneath the cliffs at Coogee. Ley fled to England where he set up illegal gambling. In 1946 he had a man murdered because he suspected he was having an affair with his mistress. He escaped the death penalty on the grounds he was insane, and died in Broadmoor asylum.

But Ley first met his match in young William Ross, a future general secretary of the Knights of the Southern Cross.

As the years went along, the Knights pioneered aged care through

Southern Cross Homes, at the instigation of Cardinal Gilroy.

The movement quickly spread to country towns where to this day it provides a spiritual and practical backbone to the KSC whether chopping wood for nuns or helping on drought and flood relief and suicide prevention.

It is a far cry from the days when Sir Henry Parkes said he wore a gun to protect himself from Catholics, when politicians claimed there was going to be Catholic Takeover of Society, as in Ireland.

We cannot live in the past lest we become like potatoes – the best part of us is under the ground. The fight against sectarianism drove us then – what drives us now?

Perhaps it is a war against relativism where in the postmodern times anybody's opinion is as good as another's. Or is it defending the Pope and Church against religious hyperbolists whatever direction they come from? Is it a war against consumerism, where everything is to be used up, including people? Or is it a struggle for recovery, to win back the hearts and minds of young people, listening to them, respecting them and giving them their place in the sun? Perhaps the critical word here is listening. Let us say the word again, Listening.

by James Dominguez*

On receiving the invitation to address the Australian Catholic Historical Society on the history of the Order of Malta, I was both honoured and daunted. Why?

The Society within the cultural life of the Church is a very august organisation with a proud heritage – now more than 70 years old and under the patronage of the Cardinal Archbishop of Sydney. It is also a respected and revered custodian of Australian Catholic tradition.

Having accepted the invitation, an early challenge was that of limiting the length of my paper. How does one condense the history of a church/ state institution, which has enjoyed a distinguished lineage for almost ten centuries, into a thirty minute address?

A Unique Institution

Let me start with some brief background on the Order, before I embark on this history odyssey.

The Sovereign Military Hospitaller Order of St John of Jerusalem of Rhodes and of Malta (or the Order of Malta as it is more usually known) has a unique status within the Catholic Church. It is of hybrid nature – a religious body but with its members - lay persons, men and women or Knights and Dames - being non-religious.

Established in mediaeval Jerusalem by a Benedictine – the saintly Frà Gerard –around 1048 to run a hospice for pilgrims to the Holy Land, it is a religious entity with its international membership today made up of eminent practising Catholics who have made a contribution to church and state.

True – it does have official chaplains as religious advisers and they too are embraced within the Order, but their status is different to that of the Knights and Dames. In Australia the Order, as elsewhere, has an active relationship with the Church and with those cardinals, archbishops, bishops and priests who are chaplains to the Association.

Over its long history, its members have pursued two goals: Tuitio Fidei, (the

---

* Jim Dominguez was a stockbroker and investment banker, Chairman of St Vincent's Public Hospital in Sydney, presently a member of other boards and a Papal Knight Commander of the Order of St Gregory the Great. He is also Ambassador for the Order of Malta to SE Asia and the Far East. This talk was given to the Australian Catholic Historical Society on 9 Oct 2011.

Journal of the Australian Catholic Historical Society 31/2 (2010/11), 95-107.

95

protection of the faith) and Obsequium Pauperum (aid to those in need). Of course these two aims merge together in practice. While this history of the Order will have a focus on Obsequium Pauperum, such must be viewed through the ever-present prism of Tuitio Fidei.

That the Order is an integral part of the Catholic Church is reinforced by its links with the Holy See, from its early days through to the present. The 12th century Papal Bull - see more below - conferring sovereignty on the Order underlines the support from Rome from early times. Over the centuries, there have been many popes who were Knights of Malta. These included in more recent times John XXIII and Benedict XVI. There have also been a number of other important institutional links enduring still today with the Holy See and the Papacy.

The Order's 11th century establishment has meant that it enjoys a seniority in time to other western rite Catholic religious orders, with the exception of the Benedictines and the Augustinians. Bodies established after the Order of Malta include the Franciscans – founded in 1209 – and the Society of Jesus – the Jesuits – established in 1540.

An Acknowledgement

I wish to gratefully acknowledge an indebtedness to the erudition of my Confrere Sir James Gobbo for making available to me his earlier scholarship. Any errors however in my text are completely of my doing.

Jerusalem

In 1048 although Jerusalem was under Muslim control it was still possible for Christian pilgrims, with difficulty, to visit the Holy Land. Some merchants from Amalfi who had trading interests in Palestine and Asia Minor paid for the building of a hospice there for pilgrims. Amalfi, along with other city states Venice and Genoa then controlled much of the trade between the East and Europe.

At that time, at least so far as Europe was concerned, there were few hospitals providing medical treatment as we know it today. There were hospices certainly which were essentially places where food and shelter were provided. The limited role of a hospital was to change under the Order in Jerusalem, partly due to the influence of Greek doctors and the more advanced Byzantine tradition of organised hospital care.

After the armies of the First Crusade captured Jerusalem in 1099, the existing hospital infrastructure grew considerably and could soon accommodate some 2,000 persons. In many respects the Hospital was very avant garde. There was a separate bed for each person and the bed linen was changed regularly. By contrast, even into the 1700's, it was common for hospital patients in Europe to sleep three to a bed.

The Order's Hospital in Jerusalem after 1099 had two physicians and two surgeons in full time attendance. It was to be a long time before hospitals in Europe had permanent medical staffing as a matter of course. In feudal times, doctors were generally not part of the staff of a hospital and they only provided treatment on an irregular basis to patients. Indeed, even a well known hospital like St Bartholomew's in London, as late as the 18th century had doctors calling only once a week.

It needs to be remembered that although the Catholic Church became very active in health care, it did not unequivocally foster the practice of medicine. In the 11th century it prohibited post-mortem examinations. As one historian put it, "the practice of surgery was left to uneducated itinerant bone setters, oculists and cutters of stone".

Voltaire ever cynical and definitely not a Hospitaller or Knight of Malta was centuries later to describe medicine as, "the art of amusing the patient while nature cures the illness".

As indicated, Frà Gerard had been in charge of the Hospital in Jerusalem from around 1048. With the capture of Jerusalem in 1099 by the Crusaders, there was a formalising of his group of committed workers who pledged themselves to follow certain religious principles and to work for the Hospital. They became known, not surprisingly, as Hospitallers. Their worthiness was formally recognised in 1113 by Pope Paschal II in a Papal Bull (a form of letters patent or decree) as an independent religious order of the Church, thus conferring a sovereignty which is still in force today.

The early novice Hospitaller had to commit to a set of rules and to confirm that he was not married nor in debt, nor subject to any other lord – or to another order. At a later date distinctions of noble birth became all important with the move into military activities - traditionally linked to knightly endeavours. The family tree was carefully investigated before a candidate could be considered for membership. (This practice still largely survives in Europe where aristocratic lineage has been seen as a condition of membership of the Order.)

Upon admission the novice swore to live and die in the service of the Order, in chastity and without personal property, and to regard the sick and the poor as his lords and masters. It was a hard oath for a young man often of wealth and nobility to take but it has to be seen in the context of his religious faith. The commitment was taken seriously and rigorously enforced.

Therefore, the Order which Blessed Gerard founded was quite revolutionary in its day for its members were required to treat the sick and the poor "as our lords, whose servants we acknowledge ourselves to be". This was a remarkable rule in the 12th century when the then known world was still based on the feudal concept of lord and serf.

Soon after 1099 the Hospitallers had hospitals also at the main pilgrim embarkation ports in the Mediterranean such as Marseille, Messina and Bari. The Hospitaller Order of St John, as it became known, grew rapidly. Indeed the 1113 Papal Bull recites that the Order was confirmed in the tenure of "all its honours and possessions" with properties in Pisa, Bari, Otranto, Taranto and Messina.

Military Role of the Hospitallers

Some fifty years after foundation, the Hospitallers developed a military capability. This was required largely because of the need to defend their presence in Palestine against the increasingly hostile Islamic warlords. This hostility had intensified because of the sack of Jerusalem in 1099 and the behaviour of the Crusaders after the city fell to them.

At that time all members of the Hospitaller Order swore the three oaths - poverty, chastity and obedience - a characteristic of religious orders even today. Their discipline then was strict and although all of them became soldiers they continued to care for the sick in their hospitals.

Eventually the Muslims recaptured Jerusalem and regained control of the whole of Palestine and Syria. In 1291 the Knights Hospitaller were obliged to leave Jerusalem.

Rhodes

From 1309 Rhodes was to become the new home for the Knights who were now a naval as well as a military power. From Rhodes they could maintain links with the cities of Asia Minor and also harass Muslim shipping. Rhodes had a good harbor, its land was fertile and it had ample forests to supply timber for shipbuilding.

The Knights however were never to lose sight of their Christian faith and origins plus their primary role as Hospitallers. It was to be an important element of their survival for it meant that in spite of occasional military setbacks they still generated spiritual and financial support.

On Rhodes the Knights continued their ministration to the poor through hospital work. The hospital constructed by them in 1478 is still substantially intact and is now the Archaeological Museum. It was in advance of any hospital then to be found in the West.

On admission to the Hospital the patients were required to bathe, confess and make their wills before the Prior. They were not permitted to disobey the orders of the physicians, or to change the prescribed treatment, but were always treated with respect. Irrespective of means they all had their own bed, protected by curtains, and might choose their food which was served as in the past from silver vessels. Both these measures were very significant and not just because they represented a departure from the accepted norm in Europe. Individual beds and the serving of food from metal vessels and not wood were important aspects of healthcare because they minimized the danger of cross infection from contagious disease.

There were several important medical measures introduced in Rhodes, including under Grand Master d'Aubusson (1503-1512) a health commission. Its membership consisted of Knights of the Order and citizens of the island as well as physicians and apothecaries from the Hospital. During plague epidemics a strict quarantine was enforced. All persons who had been exposed to the disease were isolated for a period of forty days (reputedly the origin of the term "quarantine"). If the exposure had been through their fault, a fine of 50 ducats was levied.

Organisation of the Order
It was during the Rhodes period (1309-1522) that the Knights settled on a more formal organisational structure. Members of the Order who came to Rhodes from all over Europe were from the beginning of the fourteenth century grouped according to the language spoken. There were thus, initially, seven such groups or Langues (Tongues): Provence, Auvergne, France, Italy, Aragon (with Navarre), England (with Scotland and Ireland) and Germany. In 1462 Castile and Portugal separated from the Langue of Aragon and formed an eighth Langue.

The Order as a sovereign entity was ruled then and now by the Grand Master. The Sovereign Council of the Order for a long time minted its own currency and maintained then and now diplomatic relations with other states. His Highness the Grand Master was titled Prince of Rhodes, as later he was Prince of Malta. The high officers of the Order were selected from different Langues or political states as is still effectively the case today.

The defence of particular portions of the walls of Rhodes, which were about three kilometres in length, was allocated to individual Langues. Each had an auberge or inn which was its meeting place. These are well preserved in Rhodes today. Most are in a winding avenue known as the Street of Knights and each has its own coat of arms conspicuous on the façade of its premises. I recommend a stroll down this "memory lane" which walk I did some decades ago.

The Knights always aspired to return to Palestine and at their zenith on Rhodes they controlled much of the seaways plus major cities in Asia Minor and many of the islands around Rhodes.

One of the best preserved examples of the Order's physical presence on the nearby eastern coast of what is now Turkey is the Castle of St Peter at Bodrum. The Castle was constructed by the Knights and is today substantially as they left it when they had to pull back in the face of Muslim aggression. . The walls of the Castle bear the coats of arms of members of the Order and of their patrons. This is especially evident on the English Tower which was built as a result of gifts made by King Henry IV of England and certain English nobles such as the Earl of Arundel, brother of the Duke of Norfolk.

Once the Turkish Moslems had conquered the walled city of Constantinople (today Istanbul) in 1453, it was only a question of time before they sought to capture Rhodes.

In 1522 Suleiman the Magnificent assembled an enormous army and navy and laid siege to Rhodes. His forces arrived in 400 ships with a reported troop force of 100,000 men. The assembling and supply of the large besieging force was not difficult for the Muslims since Rhodes was only 30 kilometres off the coast of Turkey. The fortifications of Rhodes had been increased by the Knights. They were only about 500 in number, supported by about 1,500 mercenaries and were greatly outnumbered. The siege lasted four months.

Eventually the Knights were forced to agree to surrender. In 1523 they were allowed with full military honours to leave in their ships with all their followers and possessions on the understanding they would no longer wage war against Islam. It was a promise that they were to break. Some 4,000 residents of Rhodes exited with the Knights. Amongst the possessions taken were precious relics of the Order and the much venerated spiritual art work icon of the Virgin Mary from the mountain shrine at Philerme (Filerimos) some fifteen kilometres from the city of Rhodes. According to legend, the image of the Virgin of Philerme (still an important and revered icon of the Order today) was painted by St Luke the Evangelist.

Malta

With their expulsion in 1523 from Rhodes the Knights having been a sovereign power in Rhodes now once again found themselves momentarily without a home. In 1530 they were granted the islands of Malta and Gozo by Charles V, the Holy Roman Emperor upon the insistence of Pope Clement VII. The Deed of Donation by the Emperor is in the Archives of the Order of St John in the National Library in Valletta. It is a superb example of the art of the legal conveyancer. It recites that the gift is made so that the Knights "should no longer be compelled to wander the world". It provided that the Knights were to pay as a due a falcon, to be presented to the Emperor each year on the Feast of All Saints. It also established that the Order should remain neutral in any war between Christian nations.

The Knights became the Sovereign Government of Malta. Consistent with their spirituality and defence of the faith they also continued via their traditional Hospitaller involvement the care of the sick and the poor. This was to be combined with a military and naval focus on the Muslims. It was again only a question of time before Suleiman responded to the mounting interference by the Knights' maritime forces with his trade and shipping in the Mediterranean.

There followed in 1565 the Great Siege of Malta, arguably one of the most famous and best recorded martial exercises in history. The Siege lasted from May to September in that year. Despite much loss of life, the defenders held firm and the Islamic forces finally withdrew. This represented the first major defeat for the Ottoman Empire for hundreds of years. If Malta had fallen, it would have given the Muslims strategic control of the Mediterranean and threatened Christendom. Their defeat marked the commencement of their decline.. Not long after, in 1571, in the famous Battle of Lepanto, the Turkish Muslim fleet was destroyed by superior forces which included the galleys of the Order.

The Great Hospital in Valletta

After the historic victory of Lepanto, the Knights made Malta their then undisputed home. They built a beautiful new city, Valletta. It was richly endowed with beautiful churches and named after Jean de Valette, the Grand Master at the time of the Great Siege. St John's Co-Cathedral is a gem of Baroque art and architecture. It was built as the conventual church for the Knights. The Grand Masters and other Knights donated gifts of high cultural value and made enormous contributions to enrich it with only the best works of art. Above all, the Knights continued their commitment under Obsequium Pauperum to the care of the sick and constructed the Great Hospital, which once again was ahead of its time.

As a brief aside it is of interest to note that the Great Hospital with its proximity to Turkey was to be utilized some 241 years later in the treatment of seriously injured Australian and New Zealand troops evacuated from the beaches of Gallipoli.

The building later to be known as the Holy Infirmary is still intact although now no longer used as a hospital. It was 155 metres long, airy and spacious. Each patient had a separate area with his own bed and mosquito netting. When not at sea or on active service , the Knights were obliged to tend to the patients and serve their meals. All eating and drinking implements were made of silver, "not for ostentation but for decorum and cleanliness".

The Infirmary was adorned by a series of paintings by Mattia Preti depicting episodes in the Order's history. He was an Italian painter of standing who spent some years on Malta carrying out commissions for the Order. Even more distinguished was the great Caravaggio allegedly a Knight of Malta who took refuge in Malta following a serious criminal charge in Rome. His great masterpiece "The Beheading of St John the Baptist" (the patron saint of the Order) and other works still hang today in the Cathedral in Valletta.

Part of the Order Hospital was a "ronta" or wheel in a contiguous building. It consisted of a room with a large rotating bed, communicating with the road outside through a discreet opening in the wall. Through this window unwanted or illegitimate babies (then called foundlings) were discreetly left on the bed from where the Infirmary staff collected them and cared for them. The entire apparatus was built in such a way that the person depositing the infant could do so without being seen from inside and thus without revealing any identity. The children were kept there until foster mothers could be found for them. Records reveal that in 1787 and 1788, 212 babies were admitted. The Infirmary also offered hospitality to many pilgrims travelling to the Holy Land. They were given food and shelter and passages were sought by them on ships directed towards the East.

In 1676 the Holy Infirmary founded the University School of Anatomy and Surgery in Malta which was to become one of the most famous in Europe. The study of anatomy was made compulsory for all medical students and they regularly had to attend lessons and demonstrations on the dissection of cadavers. In order to facilitate this study, it was determined that the bodies of patients who had died in the Infirmary could be dissected by the senior anatomy teacher. At that time, such an opportunity for studying anatomy was rare.

An early account of the Holy Infirmary was depicted in a chronicle of March 1687 by an emissary of His British Majesty, who said: ".... passing through the gate, I went around the Pharmacy, which was very well stocked. Then I visited the Doctors' rooms and entered the Square Courtyard. An intense perfume permeated it! There was a garden of oranges and lemons. From here I passed into another Courtyard which, in turn, had a certain number of citrons, and their sweet fragrant perfume wafted freshly in all the rooms arranged around it. Although there were numerous patients the atmosphere was pleasant, sweet and clean... All the patients were served by Knights with silver plates ...."

The Infirmary was staffed by a well qualified medico-surgical group. In 1725 the records indicate that the professional personnel included three senior physicians, three junior physicians, three senior surgeons, two junior "experienced" surgeons and six medical practitioners and a phlebotomist, with two assistants, "applying leeches, cataplasms and vesicants". The nursing staff consisted of a certain number of "servants or guardians" but as before the food was distributed and served by Knights and novices who looked after the sick during meals.

As the power of Islam waned, so also did the relative importance of the military standing of the Knights of Malta - as they were known - for there was less pressure on them to maintain their soldierly regimen and discipline. By 1798 when Napoleon's fleet came to Malta on the way to Egypt, the Knights were not able to repeat their great deeds of the past against the Muslims and Malta surrendered. Napoleon took away the treasures of the Knights including all the bullion and silver plate. Almost all went to the bottom of the sea along with most of his ships at the Battle of the Nile where Nelson scored a great victory.

The British then seized Malta and, in breach of the Treaty of Amiens of 1802, failed to return it to the Knights. The British held Malta until the Maltese secured their independence in1964.

After Malta
With the fall of Malta in 1798, the Order was, once again, without a home for nearly 40 years. The Tsar of Russia sought to capture the Office of Grand Master in 1801 and to appoint himself to the position. The Tsar's action was

entirely invalid and contrary to the Order's Rule. He was not Catholic; he was not celibate; he was not elected by a duly constituted meeting of the Order and his so called election was never approved by the Pope.

In 1834 the Order was re-established, in Rome where it has remained ever since. There it has its international headquarters, enjoying extra-territorial status. The Grand Magistry, where the Grand Master as Prince of the Order officially resides, is in the Palazzo Malta on Via Condotti, some 200 metres from the Spanish Steps.

The original Hospitaller missions – Tuitio Fidei linked with Obsequium Pauperum - became once again the principal focus and activity of the Order and at the end of the 19th century, a significant revival of the Order of Malta began. This was based not on any military or naval role but on that which had always been the primary justification for the Order, namely the care of our lords the sick.

False Orders

There is not sufficient time to fully discuss a different issue which has emerged in recent centuries, namely the many unauthorised or un-recognised "chivalric" orders of St John, most of which claim some identification with the Order of Malta or its history. There are a large number of such orders, including several in Australia. Using symbols and names not unlike those of the Order, they attempt to pass themselves off as the Order of Malta. Caution should be exercised in any contact with individuals purporting to do so. In some cases they may have undertaken useful charitable work but in some overseas locations they have been fronts for disreputable, even criminal organisations.

By contrast there are several orders which are recognized including those of Papal Knighthood. Others include The Equestrian Order of the Holy Sepulchre of Jerusalem. This body does not have sovereignty. Another such body is The Venerable Order of the Hospital of Saint John of Jerusalem which runs the St John Ambulance Corps in many places around the world. This body was founded in England in the 19th century and is recognized by the Order of Malta. There is today a fraternal relationship between the two organisations.

The Order of Malta Today

It is appropriate to describe briefly the current membership and government of the Order.

There are over 12,000 members of the Order in some 59 countries. As indicated earlier, the qualifications for membership are, in summary, that the candidate be a practising Catholic and have a record of community service, including a commitment to the work of the Order. Membership is by invitation not application. Admission is determined by the Sovereign Council in Rome. As a member of a religious order, Knights and Dames of the Order are still required to focus on spirituality in their day-to-day living as well as on the concomitant Hospitaller or humanitarian role. New members of the Order are reminded at their Investiture that they are joining a religious Order which requires a serious and practical commitment to their Catholic faith.

The essential government of the Order has not changed much over the centuries. Certain senior offices, including that of the Grand Master, can only be occupied by professed religious who take the three traditional vows which had formerly been taken by all members of the Order. Membership of the governing body, the Sovereign Council, is truly international.
There have been two significant changes however in membership in the last century.

In the 1920's it was agreed that candidates at least in the New World did not have to demonstrate nobiliary proofs. A proportion of the Order is thus now composed of members of Magistral Grace. In other words, they are admitted at the discretion of the Grand Master.

The other important change which followed the decline of the military role is the welcoming of women to the Order as Dames. In the tradition of humanitarian or hospitaller service and reflecting modern society the Dames play a vital role working alongside the Knights in the delivery of aid.
The Order's Sovereignty Today

The Grand Magistry of the Order continues to be responsible for the international governance of the Order and for its Sovereign and diplomatic role. The Order as a sovereign entity in international law since 1113 is presently recognised by 104 states and supranational agencies with which it enjoys diplomatic or official relations, usually with an exchange of ambassadors. Among the most recent linkages are those with Canada, Russia and Timor-Leste. The number of states with which the Order enjoys relations has doubled since 1995, thus demonstrating that over nearly 10 centuries of existence its vigour and dynamism has been maintained. There is a strong diplomatic presence throughout Latin America and the African continent.

The Order enjoys Permanent Observer status with missions at the

United Nations in New York, Geneva and Vienna. It is also linked through aid disbursement and otherwise with a number of supra-national bodies such as the European Union, WHO and UNESCO. The Order's diplomatic network facilitates the emergency aid role with an ability to work at the UN and elsewhere on a government-to-government basis and thus respond quickly when disaster strikes.

Humanitarian Aid

The Order carries out much of its work in the Hospitaller tradition at a regional level mainly through its national associations. It has a part time labour force of some 80,000 skilled volunteer staff ready to be called upon at short notice plus a full time corps of some 20,000 doctors, nurses and paramedics. Its work includes the conduct of leprosaria, hospitals and infirmaries, help to the aged, and the distribution of emergency aid to disaster-stricken countries.

A very significant recent development was the establishment in 2005, out of the Order of Malta Hospitaller arm in Germany, of Malteser International as an NGO entity. MI has quickly achieved international status as a professional deliverer of emergency humanitarian aid and has been active across the world including in the SE Asian region. It was very occupied for instance in providing relief following the 2004 tsunami especially in Aceh Province in Indonesia and in Thailand, Sri Lanka and southern India. It was also active in Myanmar after Cyclone Nargis and more recently with the Order in Cambodia and Thailand in flood relief.

MI and the Order itself are often used as conduits for the distribution of aid money by governments and supranational bodies. This entrusting of public money testifies to the professionalism, efficiency, accountability and transparency of the operations of both bodies.

Order Aid within an Australian and SE Asian Context

Over the last decade both the Order and MI have been the recipients of funds on different occasions from AusAID, the Australian Government aid agency.

The Order in Australia has liaised with MI in its Hospitaller role. The Australian Association's humanitarian effort is visible not only domestically but with near neighbours such as Papua New Guinea and The Solomons. In Timor-Leste it has been responsible for the re-establishment of a Dili ambulance corps and the linked training by the Australian Catholic University of ambulance paramedics. It is pursuing actively an involvement in several other Hospitaller roles including palliative care and maternal health in concert with the Timor-Leste Ministry of Health. It is also in dialogue with the Catholic Church there on these health issues.

Asian Expansion

A feature of the Order in Australia – established in 1974 – has been a strong focus on Asia over the last decade. The Australian Association enjoys the benefits from the linkages of the Order's diplomatic relations with a number of SE Asian states including Cambodia, Thailand, The Philippines and more recently with Timor-Leste.

The development of a presence for the Order on the ground in the region was a responsibility entrusted to the Australian Association by Sovereign Council more than a decade ago. A new Order Association was established in Singapore in 2005 initially as an Australian Delegation. Steps are quite advanced under Australian auspices for an Order presence in Hong Kong and Thailand with other countries in the immediate region also under active consideration.

Conclusion

This short history of the Order shows an organisation possessing from its foundation in 1048 very strong and enduring values. It has a tradition and a record of tenacity and of triumphing over adversity, ever renewing itself in a way that is both faithful to its original Hospitaller role and relevant in current society, always true to the principle of "Modern by Tradition".

Patrick O'Farrell and the Patrick O'Farrell Memorial Lecture

by John Gascoigne*

The institution of the Patrick O'Farrell memorial lecture thanks to Ronan McDonald and the Irish Studies Centre recognises the considerable contribution of Patrick O'Farrell to this university and the writing of Australian history and history more generally. Patrick was one of the select band of Australian historians who have left a lasting mark on our understanding of our own history. By focussing on the Irish contribution he brought out the extent to which Australian society has been from 1788 onwards plural with no one culture having the exclusive right to represent what the nation stood for. In a sense, Patrick provided the historical foundation for some of our current notions of multiculturalism with his insistence that the Irish element meant that Australia could not simply be regarded as a distant carbon copy of Britain; that the need to accommodate the pluralism that came with some one third of Australians being of Irish descent helped stimulate the growth of a distinctive Australian national identity.

Patrick was well aware, however, that accommodating the Irish element in Australia came at the price of considerable contention, even though this was accommodated in a nation which had moved away from any notion of a confessional state. His posthumous book which his daughter, Clare, has edited and placed on a website[1] -- which the O'Farrell family have established in his memory -- dealt with the vexed subject of sectarianism and has as its title, Imagination's Stain. Though written at a time when Patrick had to deal with much illness it has many of the distinctive Patrick qualities. It is written with literary flair and with an eye for the striking phrase. The chapter on the origins of sectarianism in Anglo-Irish relations going back to the Middle Ages opens for example with the phrase, 'Greed and power dressed in acquired religious robes'. It reflects Patrick's broad historical frame of reference which, as this chapter indicates, took him well beyond these shores to the cultural forces which had shaped the neo-European settler society of Australia. His eye for the major intellectual forces at work

---

* John Gascoigne is Scientia Professor of History at the University of New South Wales. This address was given on his behalf at the inaugural Patrick O'Farrell Memorial Lecture, delivered at UNSW on 9 Nov 2011 by Professor David Fitzpatrick.

in Western society is apparent in his sections on the Enlightenment and the earlier one on the Reformation with his deft summation of the sectarian differences. Above all this posthumous work reflects his passionate belief in the life of the mind and the way in which history — which he here defines as 'that branch of analytic knowledge and disciplined scholarship which deals with past time' — provides a way of understanding both ourselves and our neighbours better. For, as he insisted, the issues with which he was dealing 'live on, inextricably enmeshed in the culture, in the social, economic, political, psychological and emotive aspects of human reality.'

As a teacher as well as an author he sought to instil his conviction that history mattered. We were colleagues from the time I joined UNSW in 1980 and I saw him from many different vantage points from being on the other side of the table from him in my interviews for tutor and lecturer and, sadly, being the then Head of School when I attended his funeral and, subsequently, wrote his obituary for the university paper. What Patrick imparted to the School of History was a sense of the importance and dignity of intellectual life. This could take many forms: from persuading fledgling students at Open Days of the worth of an arts degree whatever their ultimate career path to probing questioning at a seminar. Patrick was not afraid of challenging what he considered stifling orthodoxies or of being a lone voice. He was always his own man but with a strong sense of vocation as someone who sought to persuade his fellow historians and the larger world that rigorous intellectual discussion was one of the foundations of a good society. Patrick also insisted that history should be written to be read and his work set an example for historical writing that was both accessible and rigorous. The institution of this memorial lectureship provides an opportunity to reflect and build on his legacy.

---

[1] http://www.patrickofarrell.com/

Kevin Friel* (with James Franklin)

What a difference fifty years makes.

I am in both these photos. On the far left of the 1950 scene, I am a nineteen-year-old and impressionable newly-professed Marist brother at our Bondi Beach school, St Anne's. Older and wiser, I am in the front row third right of centre in the large group of staff of Trinity Catholic College Auburn in 2000.

I may have changed in a few ways – not quite the same spring in the step, perhaps, but with a repertoire of tricks to keep a step ahead of a bright maths class. But as the photos show, it was the world of Catholic education that had changed almost beyond recognition in that time.

In 1950, every teacher at St Anne's was a brother, and we did everything ourselves. A typical day went something like this, as I remember:

5.25 wake

Reading in Latin from the book of "Little hours"

Community mass

Breakfast in silence

8.30 start teaching (preparation was done the night before)

Lunch (20 minutes each so we could cover playground supervision)

More teaching (no free periods)

After school, sports supervision was common, though I did some walking nearby and tennis (with other brothers) instead

Dinner

An hour or so for marking and lesson preparation; some spiritual reading and perhaps some letter writing to family.

---

* Br Kevin Friel (1930-2011) was a Marist Brother with an outstanding record as a teacher of mathematics. He won a Catholic Education Office Executive Director's Award for Excellence in 2006. A tribute to him appears in the NSW Legislative Assembly Hansard of 11 Aug 2011.

Journal of the Australian Catholic Historical Society 31/2 (2010/11), 110-112.

110

Some of us fitted in university study at night (without any reduction in teaching load). The brothers maintained silence except at meals; except for those of us studying outside, we rarely had occasion to speak to other adults either. Socialising with outsiders was very rare. We did have a housekeeper to cook and do laundry, but that was it for "support staff": any work that had to be done in the school itself (including cleaning), we did it. In any case, there would have been no money to pay for any staff, as there was no government aid from State or Commonwealth. Holidays,...? "Free time" often meant no more than a visit to the barber's. Our days were laid out exactly, and what to think and teach in them were laid out in rules too. We taught the 300 or so pupils Religious Education every day, and what we taught them was as clearcut as the timetable. We Catholics were on the safest train to heaven, with an infallible Pope at the controls.

Move forward fifty years. Massive changes in society – secularization, growth in population and technology, more positive attitudes to the individual but less positive ones to permanent commitment – were reflected in the schools. Trinity Catholic College, Auburn was a huge operation with 1400 students and a staff of 121 in various specialist roles – as well as teachers there were secretaries, counselors, teachers' aides, lab assistants, librarians, accountants, gardeners, and so on. There were only six brothers, none of us exactly on the young side. The lay staff of course lived outside, with family obligations and were employed under normal award conditions, so slave labour was out. State Aid comprised most of the School budget, so it was possible to pay for those civilized conditions. Religious education was less dogmatic in style. The safe train had stopped decades ago; Catholics had disembarked and were continuing the journey with sensitivity to others' religious beliefs.

I was happy in 1950 and I was happy in 2000.

In some respects, the new ways were better. People were professionally trained for their roles in ways that make our attempts at "on the job" learning in 1950 look dangerously amateur. The transition to a lay staff worked well. Sometimes a religious trained a lay person to take over. Some of the most inspirational leaders in Catholic schools were ex-religious.

But had we lost something from the old days? There was a difference in scale that meant something for the kind of education students received. Then, there were only 3000 or so students doing the Leaving Certificate. They were children of Depression-era parents and valued results as a way out of dead-end jobs. Real one-on-one teaching was possible for those in the

Marist Brothers' community, Bondi Beach, 1950

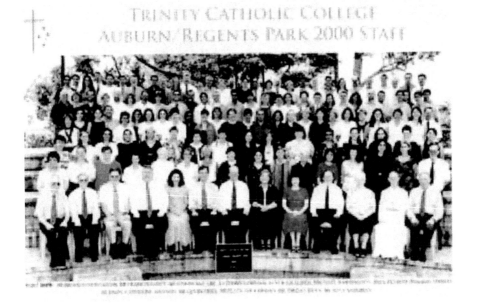

Staff of Trinity Catholic College, Auburn, 2000

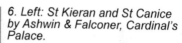

6. Left: St Kieran and St Canice by Ashwin & Falconer, Cardinal's Palace.

8. Right: St Bartholomew by John Hardman & Co., Cerretti Chapel.

7. Above: Detail of St Kieran by Ashwin & Falconer, Cardinal's Palace.

9. St Columba by Stephen Moor (attributed), Springwood.

10 Church of Mary Immaculate and St Athanasius, Manly.

11. St Columba's High School, Springwood.